APPRECIATED BRANDING

APPRECIATED BRANDING

*Transform Your Brand from
Ignored to Irreplaceable*

How to Drive Growth for Mature Brands
REID HOLMES

Copyright © 2024 by Reid Holmes

Appreciated Branding™: Transform Your Brand from Ignored to Irreplaceable. How to Drive Growth for Mature Brands.

All rights reserved. No part of this publication may be reproduced, distributed, or transmitted in any form or by any means, including photocopying, recording, or other electronic or mechanical methods, without the prior written permission of the publisher, except in the case of brief quotations embodied in critical reviews and certain other noncommercial uses permitted by copyright law.

Although the author and publisher have made every effort to ensure that the information in this book was correct at press time, the author and publisher do not assume and hereby disclaim any liability to any party for any loss, damage, or disruption caused by errors or omissions, whether such errors or omissions result from negligence, accident, or any other cause. Usage or execution of the strategies and ideas contained herein without direct involvement or oversight of the author absolves author of any liability resulting from unforeseen results or financial damages.

Adherence to all applicable laws and regulations, including international, federal, state, and local governing professional licensing, business practices, advertising, and all other aspects of doing business in the US, Canada or any other jurisdiction is the sole responsibility of the reader and consumer.

Neither the author nor the publisher assumes any responsibility or liability whatsoever on behalf of the consumer or reader of this material. Any perceived slight of any individual or organization is purely unintentional.

The resources in this book are provided for informational purposes only and should not be used to replace the specialized training and professional judgment of a health care or mental health care professional.

Appreciated Branding™ is a registered Trademark of House of Holmes, LLC, US Trademark registration number: 51492143.

ISBN 979-8-89316-271-4 (Paperback)
ISBN 979-8-89316-272-1 (Ebook)
ISBN: 979-8-89316-801-3 (Hardcover)

PLEASE NOTE: No part of this book was created with ChatGPT or AI.

DEDICATION

For anyone who wants to play to win
while making a positive difference.

CONTENTS

AUTHOR'S NOTE xi
PREFACE xiii
INTRODUCTION xv

SECTION 1: THE OPPORTUNITY 1
CHAPTER 1: How It Started vs. How It's Going 3
CHAPTER 2: Has Anyone Else Found a Solution? 10
CHAPTER 3: The Unrecognized Power of Shared Values 15
CHAPTER 4: CMO – Chief Miracle Officer 19

SECTION 2: WHAT IS A BRAND TODAY? 29
CHAPTER 5: Brand Versus Product 31
CHAPTER 6: Building Brands Today 38
   CASE STUDY: Dove 43
CHAPTER 7: Brands and Revenue 55
   CASE STUDY: Izod Lacoste 55
CHAPTER 8: The Brand Appreciation Pyramid 59
CHAPTER 9: The Plateau of Indifference 67
CHAPTER 10: The Expected and The Appreciated 73

SECTION 3: WHY SHOULD PEOPLE CARE? 77
CHAPTER 11: The Heart of Appreciated Branding -
      Caring 79
   CASE STUDY: Ariel Detergent, India 83
   CASE STUDY: Ruavieja 88
CHAPTER 12: The Importance of Story 91
   CASE STUDY: Deluxe 95

SECTION 4: PUTTING APPRECIATED BRANDING INTO PRACTICE 101

CHAPTER 13: Building an Appreciated Brand.................... 103
   CASE STUDY: Liquid Death 108
CHAPTER 14: Getting Started.. 113
CHAPTER 15: How Appreciated Brands Win 120
CHAPTER 16: The Unique Emotional Solution 127
   CASE STUDY: H&R Block 129
CHAPTER 17: What a Brand Appreciation Approach
   Requires 133
CHAPTER 18: Questions to Ask to Get the Gears Turning 137

SECTION 5: WHY ALL THIS MATTERS 141

CHAPTER 19: What Do You Want? 143
CHAPTER 20: Demand More from Your Industry 149
CHAPTER 21: The Before and The After............................. 153

CONCLUSION.. 157
Acknowledgments 161
About the Author... 163

Get the FREE Appreciation Assessment!

Make more of your brand.
Make more of a difference.
Make more for your company.

FREE DOWNLOAD HERE:

www.appreciatedbranding.com

The assessment will help you understand your appreciation earning opportunities. The result will be a stronger brand and business.

Take it yourself, ask your team to take it and aggregate the results, or ask your leadership team to take it. Or all of the above.

You'll learn:

Is your brand on the **Plateau of Indifference?**
Do people care about what you say, do or solve?
Do your company values line up with your customer's values?
How can you better focus time, resources,
and budgets to drive better results?
How can you align your branding needs with the
new societal expectations in a singular, simple
construct that decreases potential missteps?

Get the insights you need to move forward.
Go to www.appreciatedbranding.com

> *"There is a finite supply of human attention."*
>
> - Tristan Harris, co-founder and President,
> Center for Humane Technology,
> former Design Ethicist, Google

AUTHOR'S NOTE

I've enjoyed a rich, rewarding, and exciting career in advertising, rising from copywriter to Executive Creative Director. I've helped brands get noticed, grow, and gain significant market share. Solving problems and watching creativity act as a force multiplier for a company isn't just gratifying, it's fun.

In almost 30 years in the agency business, I've won almost every award the self-loving industry bestows upon itself. I've done work that brought huge success to some of the biggest, most well-known brands in America. H&R Block. Burger King. The Mayo Clinic. And many others.

As the marketing and advertising business has shifted focus from creativity to data, the idea for this book began to take form. I recognized that a different approach was needed to build a brand, or to reinvent a mature brand.

I've watched as the advertising business changed around me from being about ideas, brand building, and the power of emotional connection to the practice of relentlessly interrupting people everywhere, seemingly all the time.

It seems as though the top of the marketing funnel has been abandoned. Awareness, Interest, and Desire have slid down into one big single Activation message cocktail.

Even more importantly, we borrow this world from our children. As a father, I want to leave a legacy, do some good for the world, and do my best to help others do the same.

For brands, there is immense power and potential in doing things that matter, for both the business, and those it wishes to attract. You now hold the culmination of my experiences and ideas on the subject.

For leaders who recognize and take advantage of the opportunity this book presents, I believe my ideas will help you revitalize how you build your brand – as both an unrecognized driver of growth and a force for positive change in the world we all share.

PREFACE

While data has been a boon to efficiency and targeting, it seems to have taken our collective eye off the brand ball. A strong brand is still critical to everything marketing intends to do to drive success. Need better performing activation marketing? Build a strong brand. Need to be prepared for the AI-powered storm that's coming? Have a strong brand. Want to have a more meaningful, fulfilling career? Have a strong brand. Want to make a positive impact for the world? Have a strong brand. Need to raise prices with less risk? Have a strong brand. Want to survive and thrive in the next economic downturn? Have a strong brand.

This book offers a new way to build, or rebuild, a stronger brand in the modern distraction economy. And it reveals a huge black hole of opportunity for brands that want to break out, make a difference, and grow.

INTRODUCTION

What is an Appreciated Brand?

It's a brand that earns appreciation in what it says, does, or solves to the immediate meaningful benefit of the people the brand is trying to attract, getting it more noticed, more wanted, and more valued.

Appreciated Brands experience higher performance marketing results. And the people who build them typically experience more satisfying careers.

Here's an example. In 2017, Ariel, a brand of laundry detergent in India, found a problem they could help fix. In 95% of Indian households, only women did the laundry – in addition to all the other responsibilities they now take on both in and outside the home. Ariel launched a campaign on behalf of their best customers, women, by appealing to others in the family to #ShareTheLoad.

In its first year, sales went up 76%.[14]

The product did not change. There was no sudden influx of extra media spend to help boost sales. What happened?

Women said, thank you. Thank you for recognizing a problem that needed attention. And they showed their appreciation by making Ariel the number one brand of detergent in India.

What Ariel achieved isn't a unique one-off. In fact, I believe it's a harbinger of what great marketing must become to be most effective in our distraction economy. With the right steps, it can be available to any marketer. I've laid out a framework to help brands get the kind of growth that comes from being appreciated. Particularly for mature brands who want to go from ignored to irreplaceable.

In this book, I have included many case studies, including a deeper dive on the Ariel case. And many stories from my career that helped shape this idea.

Here's a breakdown of what to expect.

SECTION 1 – THE OPPORTUNITY. *Seinfeld* character Frank Costanza (Jerry Stiller) said at the start of "Festivus" that it was time for "the airing of grievances!" Similarly, the intention in this section is to take stock of where we are as an industry and recognize the new challenges facing CMOs, CEOs, brand managers and customers.

SECTION 2 – WHAT IS A BRAND TODAY? Creating differentiation and meaning for a brand today requires a shift in mindset. So, we revisit the difference between a product and a brand and share cases that prove how brand meaning still creates larger profit potential. Also, I discuss an outcome I call **Effectiveness Stacking**, and a construct called the **Brand Appreciation Pyramid**.

SECTION 3 – WHY SHOULD PEOPLE CARE? It's the age-old challenge for marketers. When people don't care, they don't pay attention. In this section we'll explore how the key to getting customers to care in this new era of marketing saturation is to prove to them that *you* care.

SECTION 4 – PUTTING APPRECIATED BRANDING INTO PRACTICE. The principles behind Appreciated Branding are powerful, timeless and need to be heeded if you want your brand to break through and deliver better results.

SECTION 5 – WHY ALL THIS MATTERS. Brands have a huge opportunity, and I believe responsibility, to do meaningful things, solve meaningful problems, and say things in a meaningful way. As it happens, the biggest opportunity a brand has to get attention and drive growth also happens to be the best way to help make the world a better place. It's a rare win-win-win opportunity we should all embrace.

SECTION 1
THE OPPORTUNITY

CHAPTER 1

How It Started vs. How It's Going

The media interruption model was created when humans had the bandwidth to abide and mentally process "sponsored" intrusion. Today, we are interrupted and distracted everywhere, seemingly all the time.

A new and significant opportunity is here to earn attention for brands in ways that seek to earn genuine emotional appreciation.

We are the inheritors of a society built on postwar consumerism and the media interruption model. With the advent of television soap operas starting in the 1950s, engaging serialized stories were interrupted with messages about soap, and all manner of consumer products.

Thus, the grand bargain of free video entertainment, stories, sports, and news programming in exchange for sales messages from marketers was born. And the American post-war economy became the envy of the world.

Initially, exciting products were grabbing people's attention and vaulting a new generation into the consumer age. People were eager to secure the newest household appliance and the ancillary products needed to use it. (e.g., washing powder.)

These days, consumerism is different. There are myriad stores filled with shelf after shelf of me-too solutions, all solving the same problem while claiming superiority. Gunning for our hard-earned money has spread to almost every area of our lives. Many brands think they're still here to solve the same rational problem they were first introduced to solve.

Instead of trying to be louder, bigger or spending more money to be more interruptive, the smart brands are thinking about how to solve newer, bigger problems in a culture that has changed seismically and needs solutions. Those brands will be thanked, and they will be the ones winning.

The Assault on Attention

In 2007, the smart phone debuted. Looking back, what had been a limited number of places where advertising messages could be displayed – TV, print, outdoor, radio, and by then web browsers – now looks almost quaint.

The smart phone was the oil-drilling equivelent of a once-in-a-century tranche of crude oil under marketing's collective back yard. Suddenly, the empty space 15 inches in front of our noses became primo advertising real estate; an entirely new place to distract and interrupt.

There are now 7.8 billion SIM cards around the globe. As Tristan Harris of *The Center for Humane Technology* put it on a recent episode of the podcast *How I Built This*, "…what mobile phones did is they opened the attention economy. Used to be people only spent a few hours a day on computers and then they would get offline and go outside go to a movie do something else. [With the smart phone] …increasingly every moment of our lives became part of this attention economy."

We went from having places where we couldn't be targeted by marketing, to being constantly in the "buy me" crosshairs. Even worse, in the years since the smart phone was introduced, marketers have relied less and less on creativity and human insight to get our attention, and more on tracking our every move to head us off at the pass. Or in the bathroom. Or the stoplight. Or the DMV.

How many ad messages are we exposed to daily? A Yankelevich study shows the number was 5,000 in 2007. Today, it's 10,000. In such an environment, can more interruption from more marketers have the same impact as it did when the interruption model of advertising originated? I think we already know the answer.

Solving Sells

The interruption model has been ported to the internet and is now an onslaught of messaging. It's too much. So, we ignore it more than ever.

Brands that spend some of their marketing money today to proactively solve problems and add value to people's lives are getting attention, appreciation, and imbuing their brand with meaning again. What rings true is less about what you say than what you do. Which, conveniently, will give you much more meaningful things to talk about.

One quick look at a simple marketing funnel tells the story. It has been compressed, and not in a good way. It used to be that Awareness gave way to Interest. If you did your job right, Desire would follow. And finally the exchange of money for your product or service would happen. But all four of these messaging tasks have been compressed into one message and moment. No wonder marketing and marketing leaders are under seige. We're being asked to do four things at once. We have to do it in the most narrow, noisy, competitive part of the funnel. All while only addressing a small fraction of the available market.

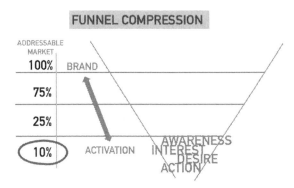

Instead of merely adding to the bottom of the funnel cacaphony, smart brands today are spending some of their marketing budgets to get attention in a new way: they're finding problems that need fixing and getting attention by helping to solve them. Consumers notice because the solutions are proactive, generous, or line up with their values.

Here's a few inspiring examples I've come across:

APPRECIATED BRANDING

In this documentary style online video, Ford in Brazil,¹ told the story of a new floor mat they developed that can also be used as an accessibility ramp for wheelchairs to go up or down curbs. Thank you, Ford.

Samsung put a camera on front of their trucks and a big screen on the back to allow would-be passers a safer view of what might be coming at them. Thank you, Samsung.

---

[1] Shannon Miller, "Ford Brazil Developed a Car Mat That Doubles as a Wheelchair Ramp," Ad week, October 29, 2018, https://www.adweek.com/brand-marketing/ford-brazil-developed-a-car-mat-that-doubles-as-a-wheelchair-ramp/.

Is Data Tracking Getting Us Off Track?

- By the time the average child is thirteen years old, the ad tech industry has collected 72,000,000 data points on them.[2]

- Over one hundred billion dollars (that's eleven zeros: $100,000,000,000) of ad spending will have been lost to fraud in 2023.[3]

- Ad professionals are always among the least trusted professions.[4]

---

[2] Geoffrey A. Fowler, "Your kids' apps are spying on them," The Washington Post, June 9, 2022, https://www.washingtonpost.com/technology/2022/06/09/apps-kids-privacy/.

[3] Rich Meyer, "Unmasking the Hidden Threat: The Escalating Battle against Online Ad Fraud," New Media and Marketing, May 17, 2023, https://www.newmediaandmarketing.com/unmasking-the-hidden-threat-the-escalating-battle-against-online-ad-fraud/.

[4] Gideon Skinner and Michael Clemence, "Advertising Execs Rank below Politicians as Britain's Least-Trusted Profession," Ipsos,

APPRECIATED BRANDING

- 81% of parents said brands care more about their data than their experience.⁵

Yay, tech?

Paul Taylor · Following
Creative Director at ADWEAK and ADWEAK STUDIO
1w · ⓢ

BREAKING: Pizza Brand Pretty Sure Since You Ordered Pizza Online Once Before That You'd Appreciate An Email Every Fucking Day

Marketers assume people will care about their product or message. But *people don't seem to care about brands anymore* because *brands don't seem to care about brand building anymore.*

If marketing were like going on a date, today we expect to skip dinner and the movie to head straight for a kiss at the door and an invitation inside for a night cap. (Or you know, a "transaction.")

Your brand identity reflects the customer relationships you build. The more value your brand offers in those relationships, the more valuable your brand becomes.

Seth Godin said: "Connect. Create meaning, make a difference, be missed."

November 18, 2018, https://www.ipsos.com/en-uk/advertising-ex-ecs-rank-below-politicians-britains-least-trusted-profession.

⁵ Maia Vines, "Parents Are Becoming More Skeptical of Brands, Study Finds," Ad Age, September 6, 2023, https://adage.com/article/agency-news/parents-are-becoming-more-skeptical-brands-mc-cann-study-finds/2514511.

CHAPTER 2

Has Anyone Else Found a Solution?

Maybe a book on this subject already existed? I looked at many of the popular books on branding from recent years and discovered a wide range of insightful and helpful resources, including but not limited to:

How Brands Grow: What Marketers Don't Know by Byron Sharp rightly and smartly splashes cold water on the long-held conventions of marketing. It is quite powerful in suggesting more empirically proven strategies, one of which is broadening reach.

Disruptive Branding by Jacob Benbunan, Gabor Schreier and Benjamin Knapp says marketers must accept the disruptive forces that are changing the world and confirms that a powerful brand is your best path to prevent being disrupted. It includes many great cases and examines many different strategies. None singular.

Building a StoryBrand by Donald Miller is probably closest to offering a single, simple, executable strategy to get noticed and build brand value based on the organizational power of story. But it seems like it's best applied to smaller, upstart brands trying to get traction.

While these books all provide powerful sources of insight for marketers, and are worth reading and having on your shelf, my aim with *Appreciated Branding* is to inspire *the immediate betterment of the brand, the business, its customers, and the world.*

The great Roy Spence of Austin, Texas ad agency GSD&M, wrote a seminal book about the importance of purpose to an organization in *It's Not What You Sell, It's What You Stand For.* As he says: "It's your reason for being that goes beyond making money, and it almost always results in making more money than you ever thought possible."

The question I was left with was the challenge of re-calibrating an entire business around a purpose, particularly a mature business with a mature brand. A company driven by purpose provides a cutting prow to the front of any organization. But it can be extremely hard to rebuild while out at sea.

Lisa Earle McLeod's *Selling with Noble Purpose* outlines the steps a company can take to recreate itself as more than an organization for profit, but as an organization that has deeper and more meaningful purpose baked into it. For any company looking to do that, Lisa's book is a great resource.

I'd be remiss if I didn't mention one of the most influential books in this genre, Anne Bahr Thompson's brilliant and insightful book *Do Good: Embracing Brand Citizenship to Fuel Both Purpose and Profit.* It wonderfully captures how companies who practice what Anne coined as Brand Citizenship get rewarded. Her 5-step model helps companies navigate how to embed social consciousness into their brand.

In a recent LinkedIn Post, Anne also discussed how brands and their leaders have significant influence in the way we all think and behave in society, as she said, "entrusting them with the responsibility to guide public discourse towards meaningful action. Yet, simultaneously,… it is imperative for marketers to navigate the delicate balance between their personal convictions and fiduciary duty to uphold a brand's values and promises."

To Anne's point, the importance of values to understand the motivating factors behind building a brand and its connection to customers is critical. In today's marketing environment where consumers can call you out very publicly, well-defined brand values will be a ready guide for marketing leaders to decide what authentic and honest efforts will not put the business at risk.

The ideas laid out in Bob Burg and John David Mann's book *The Go-Giver* are also orbiting around the concept for this book. Their central idea is based on an age-old truth that success comes from giving, from being proactive suppliers of solutions. It may best be expressed in the preface to their book written by Arianna Huffington.

> *Too often people hear "be a giver" and they think of charities and writing checks, of "giving back" once we have already done well for ourselves. But that's only a very specific facet of giving. By "be a giver," Bob and John mean be a giving person, period: one who gives thought, gives attention, gives care, gives focus, gives time and energy; gives value to others. Not as a strategy to get ahead, but because it is, in and of itself, a satisfying and fulfilling way to be.*

There is no shortage of books that spell out the importance of doing good as a human, and there is no shortage of books about the importance of brands to pursue a social mission.

It has already been proven that such efforts pay off for the business and society.

Appreciated Branding is different from all these books in that it is about practicality more than grand altruism. More about solving bigger problems in the world of your customer than in the general world at large. Spending millions to replant the rainforest is appreciated, but not as visible or immediately appreciable as spending millions to replant trees in the neighborhoods where your customers live and work.

The intersection of these two ideas is the heart of the *Appreciated Branding* platform. *A brand that is appreciated will by default, appreciate in value.*

Getting People to Care is Key

It's so key, I dedicated an entire section to it. (Section 3.) For now, it's worth reviewing some of the ways marketers try to get people to care.

1. Price. "You should care about us because our price is lower!"
2. Rational product difference. "You should care about us because our product is different and better."
3. Prolific media placement. "Care about us on your phone." "Care about us on your TV." "Care about us on the web."
4. Rewards programs. "You should care about us because we reward you with points."

5. Data tracking. "You seemed to care about us over at that other website so care about us here."
6. Search. "You care about finding a _____. Well, we're that."
7. Emotional values recognition. "Care about us because we help you solve bigger problems that matter to you."

For a brand that wants to stand out, grow, maintain profitability, build brand meaning, enjoy better activation marketing, and make a difference, number 7 should be your focus. That is the focus of this book.

CHAPTER 3

The Unrecognized Power of Shared Values

How do you break through and get noticed in the busy world of selective attention? Through the power of shared values.

Ad agency Crispin Porter + Bogusky (now Crispin+), memorably illustrated the power of values in a trade ad they ran back in the 1990s. The simple brilliance of it opens a story loop that the reader will identify with, feel an emotional response to, and care about.

The key to earning appreciation for a brand starts with building human connections with your customers. Not technological connection. Not data files. Not re-targeting media. Human connection. Humans connect emotionally to people and organizations that share and promote their values and beliefs. Values determine behavior.

Today, target audiences in marketing are still determined by demographic, generational, age-based stereotypes. Demographic targeting is like the black and white TV of the 1950s. To bring consumer wants, needs, and desires into full HD color, it's now more critical to focus on the values that large groups of people may share, regardless of age. Demographic targeting is inefficient and leaves perfectly willing and interested customers untargeted and untapped. Values-based targeting takes out the often erroneous assumptions made based on age.

In his book titled: *We're All the Same Age Now,* David Allison describes a more precise, effective, and efficient science he's developed to target consumer groups. He calls it "Valuegraphics."

According to Allison, "Valuegraphics uses big data to unlock the shared values of large groups of people." This approach is a much more quantifiable way to determine, and even predict, how your marketing effort will resonate than by the guesswork of the assumed commonalities of age. Allison continues, "It's an astonishingly effective audience profiling tool because *what we value determines what we do.*"

He has conducted many extensive studies of almost a million subjects in North America on the top values driver's humans use to make decisions. From this research, he's organized ten target groups of human populations who share the same values, each group with a descriptive label related to their human interests, not their age.

So, instead of throwing a dart at "millennials" as a broad age-based cohort, you'd be better off targeting, for example, people who value adventure, regardless of age (what Allison calls "The Adventure Club," 11% of the population who agree with each other 89% of the time.)

Or people who value relationships over material consumption ("the Anti-Materialists Guild," 13% of the population who agree with each other 85% of the time.)

Knowing the values and beliefs of targetable cohorts of people is crucial in the creation of compelling ideas that they will pay attention to, and appreciate, in their lives.

Targeting based on values and using the corresponding data to help see around the corner to effectiveness means we can better know which "half of my marketing budget is wasted," as early marketing pioneer John Wanamaker once said.

Allison's research sets the stage for a profound new era in marketing effectiveness. It allows marketers to focus their messages not just on those whose age might indicate a potential desire to purchase, but on those who share the same values and therefore, have a built-in reason to appreciate *your brand*.

Consumers knowing your brand for its name, product or logo is one thing. Consumers knowing your brand because its *behavior* supports the values they appreciate, want to live by, and cherish is quite another.

> ***"For a brand, behavior is destiny."***
> — Jim Weber, CEO Brooks Running

CHAPTER 4

CMO - Chief Miracle Officer

The number one challenge CMOs face is to "create meaningful connections with consumers," according to a recent *Forbes* article.[6] This is not surprising. What *is* surprising is how CMO's are being asked to create this connection. Data seems to have changed the definition of "meaningful." To a consumer, mere technological connection is not meaningful. Particularly when it's a one-sided, product-centered interruption.

Technological connectivity, media retargeting, and transaction harvesting have turned CMOs into Chief Sales Officers. Sales harvesting without brand meaning is unsustainable. Connecting first with potential new customers on common beliefs and values is being sidelined or ignored.

To a consumer, a meaningful connection is an *enduring* connection. A reliable connection. A trusted connection. This should be job one for a company that wants to have influence and command healthy profit margins. Funnels, after all, empty. They need constant re-filling.

---

[6] Matt Bertram, "What Challenges Will CMOs Deal with Most Often in 2022?" Forbes, April 21, 2022, https://www.forbes.com/sites/theyec/2022/04/21/what-challenges-will-cmos-deal-with-most-often-in-2022.

Forbes goes on to rank "optimizing funnels using big data" as the number two challenge. Data has helped significantly increase ROI on *known* leads. The problem, however, goes back to the first challenge. How are you refilling that funnel? How are you inviting people into your brand's world? Or better stated, what are you doing to be invited into your customers' world?

Running a performance marketing campaign may get results. But by offering consumers a reason to pay attention because they know and believe in the brand, you're turbo-charging that performance marketing with trusted recognition so it can deliver bigger results.

The third top challenge facing marketers is "retaining staff and talent." The very public efforts to generate sales have a huge effect on the culture and passions of the people in that organization. Is there meaning behind why you do what you do? Are your employees in it only for the paycheck? Or do they feel like they're a part of a bigger mission? Are you reinforcing a transactional culture with every paid ad you put out? Or are you creating a sense of belonging that makes your employees feel wanted, special, and needed?

How you communicate has a big impact on employee beliefs and morale. Live the values of the business publicly and your employees see it. If it's more transactions, they believe in being transactional. If it's meaningful and worthy of greater appreciation, they believe in something more than their paycheck.

According to *Forbes,* CMOs are rightly concerned with data privacy and security. But my guess is that they are concerned with it for different reasons than their customers.

Customers most certainly want their data to remain private. But marketers are concerned that the digital tools they use to target customers, such as cookies or pixel tracking, may go away. If you haven't built up any emotional brand meaning – the fundamental emotional connection you must have in place, regardless of format, channel, or social platform – you're at the mercy of technological connections. You're effectively renting those customers and subject to the whims of those platform owners who can change the rules on you. (Or be legislated into doing so.)

With more being asked of them and fewer resources at their disposal every year, it's no wonder they've also been called "Chief Miracle Officers." More and more, the power of branding is not leveraged. No surprise the average CMO tenure is only about two years.[7] And more headlines lately speak to the CMO role becoming extinct.

CMOs must factor so much into decisions big and small: budgeting, agency partnerships, team resource allocation, media planning and buying, creative oversight and execution. All of this in an environment where the goal posts seem to move with unpredictable regularity.

I list these things here not to remind CMOs of the *fun* they get to have every day with all this stuff – sarcasm intended – but to clearly state that I get it, that I'm aware of and empathetic to the CMO bull ride.

---

[7] Megan Graham, "Average CMO Tenure Holds Steady at Lowest Level in Decade," The Wall Street Journal, May 5, 2022, https://www.wsj.com/articles/average-cmo-tenure-holds-steady-at-lowest-level-in-decade-11651744800.

What's Keeping Marketers Up at Night:

Return on Marketing Spend (ROMS). How much waste is in your marketing spend? There's so much fraud in reporting, and data degradation is real. How do you improve your cost per acquisition confidently?

Generational change. Younger generations consume media and content with little patience for the "interruption model" of advertising. Are you building an emotional connection to compensate for their antipathy? Advertising has become so prolific, so ubiquitously interruptive, it's causing brand indifference and working against the higher business purpose of branding and brand value.

Technological change. Keeping up with new technology is a job unto itself. Is artificial intelligence or ChatGPT going to save the day, the week, or the weekend? Will it lead to a disconnect that only a human could suss out?

Absence of big, organizing brand ideas. Why should your brand matter to people? What's meaningful about it? What makes it magnetic to those you want to attract? Branding is still the best way for a company to earn higher profit margins and create long-term business value. And it's still the way consumers mitigate risking money through earned trust.

Cookie and pixel paranoia. What happens to your marketing plan when cookies go away? What happens when privacy gets legislated? What happens when the platform that just got dialed in for you releases their next updated algorithm?

Trust erosion. Social channels have all manner of sales pitches hitting your customers that are eroding trust. If you haven't established your brand as credible, you're throwing good money after bad.

Brand safety. Are any of your ads being placed in content that is contrary to your brand's values and beliefs? Real-time bidding can put your brand at risk by appearing to condone content that goes against what your brand stands for.

Personalization. When someone you know and appreciate calls you by name, it's a pleasant salutation. When someone you don't know, don't trust, or don't care to know calls you by name, it can be off-putting. How are your efforts at personalization striking your customers? Creepy and crass? Or wanted and welcomed?

Decision politics. Putting great ideas out in the marketplace takes faith, trust, and courage. When a brand's real values and beliefs are clearly defined, it's easier to reach a consensus and focus on the right path forward.

The experience economy. Are you creating experiences worth talking about? Or are you just talking about things you think will get you attention? There's a big difference. Think about it like junk content vs. nutritious content. One is helpful, appreciable and builds strength. The other is ephemeral, forgettable, and usually insignificant.

Media proliferation. The way to build and maintain a truly powerful brand has changed. Brands can command a higher price and thus provide rich margins from their few loyal, long-standing customers who repurchase regularly. But in this new splintered media saturated marketplace, meaningfully breaking through is harder than ever.

Data points, not stories. Humans have formed connections and retained memories through stories since the dawn of interpersonal communication. Today, product features and benefits can go by in a blur of bullet points.

Proactivity, unexpected problem solving, generosity, and the championing of values hasn't been leveraged by most marketers. It's a black hole of opportunity for brands.

What we really need to target are the things that are constant – **human values**. They are independent of tech platforms or content trends, and they are evergreen. The values companies and their customers share are what should inform content that will resonate.

Transaction Chasing

When a marketer chases customers to different places on the web thinking they just haven't come to their senses and finished the transaction, it can be off-putting. It's like a form of stalking. I call it **Transaction Chasing.**

If all you're doing is trying to find a buyer, not a longer-term customer relationship, then you're not building a brand. You're just the modern-day equivalent of an Amazon drop shipper, capturing margin as a middleman. You're not building emotional meaning beyond a product's basic function, you're not building much shareholder value, and you're not building differentiation.

You're probably working with rational "feature and benefit" messaging in a parity category where price is the chief deciding factor for buyers. While features and benefits are important factors, if that's all you're trading on, chances are they're not the meaningful result of the beliefs and values of the company.

These days CMOs have been forced to become transaction chasers more than brand builders. It's no wonder many companies are starting to eliminate the CMO role entirely. Fortune magazine reported recently that UPS, Walgreens, Etsy, McDonald's, Lowes, and Uber have all eliminated the role as a standalone job in favor of distributing the responsibilities across the organization.

With the job more about parsing data than earning attention and loyalty through meaningful human connection, organizations seem to be putting their future in the hands of data and AI. They're moving their marketing stacks to the IT department in the process.

It's a very different world than it was just a decade ago. In my view, while these companies may still win data or AI enabled gains, their long-term brand meaning and growth prospects will suffer.

Has Creativity Taken a Back Seat to Data?

In the Twin Cities, where I live and work, the Business Journal[8] recently published a list of the top ten largest advertising agencies. Only one of them was billed as a "creative" agency. Not too long ago, all of them were. The Twin Cities' top ten was a creative mecca, a *who's who* of internationally lauded creative powerhouses.

---

[8] Ethan Nelson, "Largest Advertising Agencies in the Twin Cities," Minneapolis/St. Paul Business Journal, August 17, 2023, https://www.bizjournals.com/twincities/subscriber-only/2023/08/17/largest-advertising-agencies-in-the-twin-cities.html.

Could this list of top agencies be a harbinger that creativity in advertising has lost its power or relevance? Every time I turn on my TV or scroll on my phone, it's one flat rational sales appeal after another. Perhaps the thinking is that merely getting a product in front of us will be enough to win us over?

A rational explanation of a new whiz-bang product with no competitor makes total sense. But rational product benefits get copied and become noise. Continuing to messsage around rational benefits thinking data targeting will save the day is short-sighted. And yet this top 10 list of agencies clearly indicates the pendulum has swung too far away from the immense power of creativity, big differentiating brand ideas, storytelling and emotional connection.

A lot of consumer behavior these days is a result of having been burned by marketing. People are asking, is that a trustworthy link? Will they use it to capture my data? Will I get a computer virus? Are you asking me for my email or cell number just to get me something for "free," or should I expect you to clog up my email box or text me to death? Or worse, sell my cell number or email address? This kind of "marketing" is hard to appreciate. It's making everyone look bad and weakening the tools we can all use.

The conclusions drawn from data can often be overly assumptive. If there is no larger meaning established to help people recognize your brand and have reason to care, you've effectively done nothing to till the soil that data may imply is rich with opportunity. That's when performance marketing becomes most expensive. The boost in effectiveness that is generated from being known and cared about is absent. As the saying goes, you can't save souls in an empty church.

As a marketer, you may be saying, "Well, I'm in B2B, all this marketing saturation is more on the consumer side." Or "B2B is very different from B2C, so this is interesting, but ultimately irrelevant to what I do as a marketer." To me, that's a dangerous position. The fact is, B2B targets are also B2C targets for other products. Anyone who is in marketing should be aware of message saturation from all fronts.

Marketing isn't really B2C or B2B, it's B2H. We're all human. The goal is to solve problems. Products and services exist to help us solve them. The venue in which purchasing decisions are made is irrelevant. People are people.

Advertising is at a crossroads.

1. Technology is enabling people to avoid advertising more than ever. You can get a Netflix account for ten bucks. Or HBO Max or Hulu or Amazon Video. In that sense, as Scott Galloway, marketing professor at NYU Stern and multiple podcast host, said at a recent conference: *"Advertising has become a tax on the poor and the technologically illiterate."*[9] Of course, the implications of such a statement include a couple things. One, that people are willing to pay money to avoid marketing. And two, those who are seeing your ads may not have the means to pay for your product or service.

2. To get noticed in this new era, you must do something worth talking about, not just say something that only promotes *your* agenda. For the CMO who isn't

---

[9] Tom Fogden, "'You're Dead in 18 Months or Less'": Scott Galloway on The Future of CMOs, accessed December 2023, https://www.bandt.com.au/youre-dead-in-18-months-or-less-scott-galloway-on-the-future-of-cmos/.

invited to influence the creation of the product or service they're asked to sell, that means finding something in the human experience your product can fix or improve that will be welcomed, wanted, and true to the values the brand and its customers share.

3. Big brand and media budgets are a great resource, but to build a resonant and sturdy brand, meaningfulness breaks through much more powerfully than endless repetition. The media ecosystem is hungry for content they can talk about, appreciate, and propagate. In that sense, the ascendance of PR cannot be overstated. The opportunity to create sharable stories that consumers will spread for you has never had more potential.

The best marketing has always required a great product, one that is worth talking about, that solves a real problem for consumers, and, in so doing, earns their trust and appreciation. Advertising has always been a fertilizer that helps those great products grow faster and bad products fail faster.

The products that survive, however, get competitors. So, they need to find a way to rise above a noisier category.

SECTION 2

WHAT IS A BRAND TODAY?

CHAPTER 5

Brand Versus Product

A product is not a brand. A product solves a rational problem. A brand solves an emotional problem.

Butch and Sundance

A story from one of my all-time favorite movies, *Butch Cassidy and the Sundance Kid*, illustrates this point; the messaging for a mere product often being mistaken as brand building. This is why a brand is, at its most basic, a trust mark. Like a known face, it's a visual cue that disarms. Expectations are known. Behavior is predictable. Not so with products from unknown entities.

A crowd of twenty or so men have gathered on the dirt-street town square across from a saloon. The town marshal is trying to recruit a posse to ride out and apprehend the thieves who just robbed the train.

As those very thieves, Butch and Sundance, (Paul Newman and Robert Redford) observe as they drink beer on a saloon deck above, the marshal passionately continues, "And so I'm asking you to join with me to end this scourge..."

Suddenly a new voice interrupts and stands up next to the marshal.

"Boys and girls, friends and enemies, meet... the future!" A salesman presents a gleaming new product. "The bicycle. Cheaper than a horse. No oats. No mess. No kicks. No bites. No runnin' away. No steppin' on your foot. Nothin' to step in."

The marshal has lost his audience to a sales pitch for an intriguing new product.

Notice a few things here about this pitch. It's explaining a new and novel *product*, called a bicycle. His pitch is to explain the product, which is required because it is unique, totally new, and never seen before. Its only frame of reference is its current competition: the horse. It has no *name,* no "brand" other than the product category it just created: bicycles.

So, the pitch for it is wholly logical, informational, and rational. It is not trying to reframe the idea of other bicycles as inferior. It doesn't need to. No other bicycle brand exists.

And yet today hundreds of marketers are spending billions of dollars to *explain their product* in categories that are not unique. The product's purpose is not newsworthy, it's in an already well-established category and the benefits are known and expected.

Imagine introducing a product in a competitive category today by merely talking about its functional, rational benefits.

"Ladies and gentlemen, as you leave the fair to get into your Tesla's, behold, the electric razor! It cuts whiskers without shaving cream! It won't cut your skin! And no dirty sink bowl to rinse! Just plug it in and use *electricity* to shave your face clean!"

You'd be lucky to have one person left over to laugh at you, let alone find a buyer. This is why the brand must uniquely differentiate itself from others in the category by reframing the customer's pain point. (More on this later.)

For now, as happens with new, unique, and novel products, the initial buyers ("early adopters") see it as an opportunity to enhance their own personal image by being the first to own an entirely new product in an entirely new category.

In the case of the bicycle, that's Butch. In the next scene, we see his head floating mysteriously past a window outside Etta Place's house.

"Meet the future," Butch says to get Etta to come outside. "Do you know what you're doing?" she responds through the window. "Theoretically," says Butch.

Next, B.J. Thomas sings Burt Bacharach's "Raindrops Keep Fallin' On My Head," as one of the most memorable scenes in cinema plays out, Butch giving Etta a ride on the handlebars of his new product: the bicycle.

Butch's bicycle at this point is merely a product. Until a competitor comes along, it doesn't need a brand in the modern sense of the word. It is new. *And new gets noticed.*

What is a Brand?

If all you're doing is asking people for their money in exchange for your product, you're a vendor. Your brand identity is not relationship oriented, it's transactional.

If, however, you do things to create meaning, champion values, and prove you stand for something, then your brand will differentiate itself in more meaningful ways. You don't always need huge amounts of money or investment to do this.

This is why my favorite definition of brand comes from Charlotte Beers, former CEO of Ogilvy, where I started my career. She once said, "a brand is created when a company EARNS the right to have a relationship with a customer."

That definition has never been truer than today. Brands become wanted because they have earned that privilege by saying, doing and solving things that earn meaningful associations for customers to want to share and believe in.

You can sell a product on features and benefits alone, but **a brand is the glue that holds together the business, and the people who love it, over time**.

Why is a brand important?

Brands give the business higher and more enduring lifetime value. Appreciated Brands are cherished brands that have more loyal followers who'll repeat purchase. Engaging an existing customer to repeat purchase is ten times more cost-effective than persuading a new customer to learn about, trust, and purchase your brand.[10]

---

[10] Danna, "How Emotional Connections Create Champions."

What's the ROI on Branding?

It's been proven that branding paves the way for sales. As a creative director, this was always our bread and butter, to define a brand as worthy of attention and consideration.

Through LinkedIn, I discovered an insightful perspective on KPIs and the impact of branding, presented by Adrian M. Peticila – someone I haven't met personally. This explanation serves as a basis for the deeper explanation that will unfold in this book.

Follow these five KPIs to measure what a brand does for sales:

Sales timeline

If prospects are familiar with your brand, your sales cycle gets shorter.

Exchange rates

As more people like and trust your brand, selling your products gets simpler.

Organic social mentions

Lean, mean, brand awareness machine.

Click-through rate

If your CTR rises, it shows consumers already recognize your brand and are more likely to click on your ads.

Branded term search volume

The higher the number, the better your results.

In short, a known brand creates a better-performing business.

And yet with the endless interruption that is marketing these days you could say AIDA (Awareness, Interest, Desire, Action) has taken on new meaning: Animosity, Intrusion, Disdain, Aversion.

For branding to regain its powerful ability to deliver on its promise, it must find a new way to be of greater value to people.

The Havas Meaningful Brands Report

Thanks to agency network Havas, we have an annual study of consumer attitudes toward the value of brands. On the surface, the news is not good. But I think it's in danger of being misinterpreted.

A few years ago, they labeled brand building as more challenging in "the age of cynicism." Today, Havas says we're living in the "me-conomy." It's clear branding has some stiff headwinds. The latest report reveals:[11]

- Consumers said: **"75% of brands could disappear and be easily replaced."** To me, this data point is not saying that brands don't matter anymore. It's

---

[11] Kyle O'Brien, "Havas Releases Latest Meaningful Brands Report on the 'Me-conomy,'" Agency Spy, May 17, 2023, https://www.adweek.com/agencyspy/havas-releases-latest-meaningful-brands-report-on-the-me-conomy/181157/.

saying that what brands are doing to try to matter isn't working anymore.

- **"71% [of consumers] have little faith that brands will deliver on their promises."** To me, this means consumers have never been more cynical about being "sold." So, the door is wide open for brands to do things that will truly matter.

- People are **"desperately seeking brands that can make a difference, with 73% who think brands must act now for the good of society and the planet."** When 73% of anything is left wanting, I mean, that's a huge, huge, huge opportunity.

- **"72% are tired of brands pretending they want to help society when they just want to make money."** Customers sniff out brands that are giving lip service to "doing good." And I'll take it one step further. Doing good for society is one thing, but finding ways to *do good for your customers*, outside of the solution of your product, is the biggest opportunity brands have in today's "me-conomy."

CHAPTER 6

Building Brands Today

> *"In a parity world, my best friend wins."*
> —Hal Riney, legendary copywriter, and creative director

More than a decade before he invented the new marketing real estate made possible by the smartphone, Steve Jobs crystalized the importance of brand meaning. It was the late 1990s after he had returned to Apple. Here's what Jobs said when introducing "Think Different:"

> *In this very noisy world, we have to be really clear about what we want people to know about us. Apple spends a fortune on advertising. You'd never know it. Our customers want to know: Who is Apple? And what is it that we stand for? Where do we fit in this world? Apple's core value is that…we believe that people with passion can change the world for the better. We believe that the people that are crazy enough to change the world are the ones who actually do.*

Apple clearly reverse engineered their very powerful campaign out of a truth about their company. They *do* think differently. The proof was already in their products. Their customers appreciated the power of thinking differently. And Apple wanted to invite more like-minded people to the fold.

What gets celebrated, confirmed, or shared by consumers is not simply what you say, but what you do. This is what makes what you say worth hearing. This builds brand reputation and strengthens the emotional connection a brand has with its customers. It's what turns a logo mark into a trust mark.

New Gets Noticed. Bothersome Gets Booted. Appreciated Gets Remembered.

Brands exist like a sandcastle on the beach that will gradually be washed away by the sea. But brands that take proactive steps to matter are the brands that endure and increase in value. They withstand the tides by saying, doing, and solving things that earn an appreciated, wanted place in people's lives.

The value of any business is directly proportional to how easy it is for people to say *yes* to what you're selling. Not easy to buy yes, but emotionally easy to appreciate yes. Removing as much mental friction as possible to get to that *yes* is the goal, and the earning of appreciation is the grease.

The extent to which your brand is appreciated will influence the following:

- Your ability to command higher prices
- Being most relevant in mature, "me-too" categories

- Galvanizing your employees and attracting higher-quality talent
- Increasing the ROI of your promotional advertising
- Retaining a growing and more devoted customer base
- The stature of your brand in society

So, let's get into each of these.

1. Your ability to command higher prices

Appreciated Brands are less price-sensitive, they are stickier, have more loyal customers, and they create more word-of-mouth buzz. It's never been more important to remember that your current customer knows your next customer. Nothing more credibly supports a higher price than a current customer justifying the worthiness of a brand to your next customer.

Appreciated Brands are also better justified to increase price if economic or business reasons require it. And in some cases, for an Appreciated Brand price is either less concerning or a desirable feature.

2. Being most relevant in "me-too" categories

Consider dishwashing detergent. Perhaps one brand decides to go create a TV commercial about the rational benefit of squeaky-clean plates. They put a multi-million-dollar media buy behind it, with a big national TV commercial.

Conversely, another brand decides to start a #rackthatdish campaign aimed at encouraging husbands to actually put a dirty glass or dish into the dishwasher instead of setting it on the counter.

APPRECIATED BRANDING

Which do you think would be more appreciated by buyers of dishwashing detergent, most of whom happen to be women? Which do you think would be more talked about? Which story do you think would get shared most?

Depending on how much money is put behind it, the "squeaky" clean plate commercial would certainly raise brand awareness, but would it inspire any kind of meaningful conversion? Any brand gets plates squeaky clean.

The brand that's championing a solution to a real problem, and showing purchasers that they're on their side, would make more waves, get more attention, and be more memorable.

Nobody is unloading their dishwasher lamenting a plate that isn't "squeaky" after it's cleaned. But when a woman witnesses her husband put a dirty glass in the dishwasher? That's a thank you.

It's the difference between reminding people you want them to buy your product and reminding people that you understand their lives and that you're meaningfully trying to help.

3. Galvanizing your employees and attracting higher quality talent

Companies that live their mission and values attract like-minded people. People with a shared mission and similar values work better together.

If, on the other hand, people are coming on board just for the paycheck, it's very likely "good enough" is part of your company's performance culture, even though you'd never put that on a break room poster. You're not doing anything special or different to inspire A players to investigate your next job opening. They want to perform at a high level, and yet you're not doing anything in your marketing to signal you care about A level performance.

4. Increasing ROI on promotional advertising

A brand that is recognized and means something simply inspires more action when it is promoted. As Les Binet and Peter Field – renowned British advertising effectiveness gurus – prove in the Dove case to follow, the right advertising spend is roughly 60% on brand and 40% on performance. This is how you maximize your marketing spend for ROI.

It can be tempting to think you'll capture more sales by going all in on "buy now" messaging. But as Binet and Field proved, it's just not as effective. People want to know your emotional drivers, values, and beliefs. Only then will they have the information to know whether they want to do business with you.

5. Retaining a growing and more devoted customer base

Generating single transactions from multiple different customers is more expensive than multiple transactions from single customers.

The latter is what Appreciated Brands enable: a larger customer base that doesn't just appreciate your product as a rational solution to a problem, but they have an appreciative bond with the brand, so they forsake other options. That bond of appreciation also turns them into an evangelist for your brand. It means that, when given the opportunity to tell a story about the product or the brand, they're more likely to do so.

6. The stature of your brand in society

Appreciated Brands tend to do better because they have achieved higher stature in society. That stature correlates with how much people want to associate with the brand; either as purchasers and supporters of the product or service, willing wearers of the logo as a representation of their values or self-image, or as people who are proud to work for the company because it raises their stature by association.

CASE STUDY: Dove

In honor of the 50th anniversary of the Effie Awards, marketing strategist, author, and contributing *Marketing Week* columnist Mark Ritson presented the Dove Effie Awarded Case Study video. In it, he used the results of the brand's "Campaign for Real Beauty" to masterfully explain the power of brand meaning to a product's sales results. He slso covered the proper balance of long-term and short-term brand spend versus performance spend.[12]

Dove is a legacy brand, a mature brand in a mature category, and although for years it was positioned as a face bar that was gentler on the skin, it was arguably a parity product with competitors who espoused the same rational cleaning benefits. When Dove was originally introduced, its initial rational USP was that it contained "1/4 moisturizing cream."

---

[12] Marketing Week, "Mark Ritson on How Dove Challenged Beauty Industry Stereotypes," June 24, 2019, YouTube video, 9:32, https://www.youtube.com/watch?v=GirRXvVUR28.

Cut to the 2000s. Nearly all brands in the beauty category were using the same marketing: standard fare of beautiful models whose porcelain-looking, blemish-free skin was made possible by [insert whatever beauty brand here].

But Dove realized, as a mature brand, they needed to create more emotional meaning to differentiate the brand, not keep harping on product benefits, however "differentiated" they may be.

Some very smart strategists realized there was an unaddressed truth, a cultural tension they could leverage. It was one the brand itself had been helping to perpetuate.

Ads in the beauty category were setting unachievable beauty expectations for women and girls, and even worse, affecting

APPRECIATED BRANDING

their self-esteem. The most glaring data point was that less than 4% of women *considered themselves beautiful*.

Dove realized they could continue to spend on this inauthentic, unattainable beauty expectation. Or they could start championing a more real, human belief system. They decided to make their brand about one central truth: Everyone is beautiful in their own way and that should be celebrated.

Dove was smart enough to realize it was a territory no other brand owned, so this unique emotional solution was theirs for the taking.

In 2004, Dove and Ogilvy launched *The Campaign for Real Beauty*. They confronted, head-on, the fact that beauty advertising was depicting totally unrealistic-looking women in their ads.

In this way, Dove established an overarching meaning for the master brand, which, in turn, earned appreciation from its customers for shunning the conventions of beauty advertising.

This also meant that when it came time for tactical performance marketing against specific Dove products, the Dove customer was more responsive because the brand had more credibility and authenticity.

In my view, it seems the brand decided they could release their customers from their near universal feeling of inferiority. They de-positioned their competitors as advocating for a definition of beauty that was simplistic, unattainable, and superficial.

Performance Marketing Suffers When Brand Identity Gets Lost

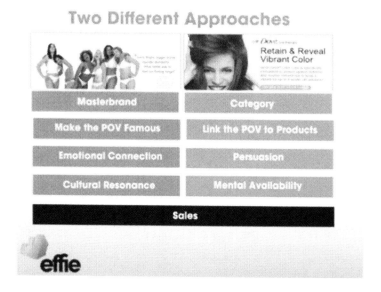

From the Effie case study, the interdependence of brand and promotion is espoused by Binet and Field, advertising effectiveness researchers known as the "grandfathers of effectiveness." Make the brand famous by resonating emotionally and culturally. Then, harvest that goodwill and appreciation to drive higher results in your performance marketing.

APPRECIATED BRANDING

In 2007, after running this campaign for 3 years, something really telling happened. Supporting that overarching brand meaning was seen as a non-ROI generating "cost."

For those who want to drive results, this is important. Dove *decreased* the Real Beauty brand messaging they had started in 2004.

The result was that sales flattened.

When they had the Nielsen company examine their Real Beauty brand campaign, it was revealed that **for every $1 they were spending on brand building, it was returning $4.42 in incremental revenue.** This proved a synergy between brand meaning and performance marketing.

In Peter Field and Les Binet's book, *The Long and the Short of It,* they proved the decisive connection between performance marketing and brand marketing. Measuring short-term marketing effects, (up to 1 year), medium-term effects, (1 – 2 years), and long-term effects, (3+ years), they set out to answer the question: how do you balance short term and long-term spending to maximize results?

What they discovered, in layman's terms, was that if you focus too much on short term performance marketing, you'll be giving up long term growth. Focus too much on brand marketing and you won't be maximizing short term sales.

Binet and Field were also out to find the correct balance of brand spending versus performance marketing spending. Performance marketing can create sales spikes, but they won't last beyond that activation spend window. But by building a meaningful brand over time each of those investments in performance marketing can be progressively more effective.

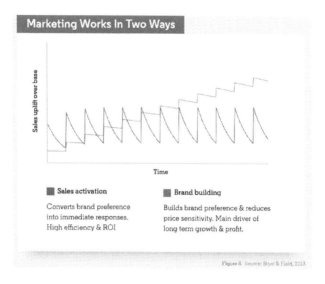

Figure 8. Source: Binet & Field, 2013

In the case of Dove, they discovered that short-term sales activation and long-term brand building *both need to work together for maximum ROI*.

Binet and Field acknowledge and indeed prescribe a balance for the highest effectiveness. They explain that there is no *long* without *short* and no *short* without *long*.

Short-Term Measurement Inhibits Long-Term Growth

As Mark Ritson said in the Dove Effie case, "The problem is most marketers in the 21st century work in a sub-12-month or sub-6-month time horizon. If you look at the world from that point of view, it looks like short-term marketing makes more sense because it gives you a better ROI. But ROI is a misleading statistic most of the time because the time variable on which it's calculated is often far too short."[13]

---

[13] Marketing Week, "Mark Ritson," 9:32.

So, the choice really is not which to do, but how much of each to do to optimize profit-generating potential.

What Binet and Field discovered was, and this differs somewhat depending on category, (I encourage you to reference their book if you want more granularity), effective marketing spend, in general, should comprise 60% of spend on brand and 40% on performance marketing to achieve maximum ROI.

Both Long & Short Combined

Brand Building	Sales Activation
Creates Brand Equity	Exploits Brand Equity
Future Sales	Current Sales
Broad Reach	Tightly Targeted
Emotional	Persuasion
Master-Brand	Product Line
60%	40%

Binet & Field, The IPA, The Long & The Short of It

Binet and Field stress that they're neither stating opinions nor just advocating for "brand." They've developed empirical evidence over twenty years of studying branding's effect on performance.

A Thought Experiment

Say Company *A* and Company *B* are two similar businesses in the same category with a similar parity product and budget. Company *A* (*A* for Activation) spends their whole quarterly marketing budget on activation marketing: email, direct mail, digital display, and retargeting.

Company B (B for Brand) embarks on a program to build (or rebuild) their brand, truly and authentically. They spend less on an activation campaign because they invest in a campaign to build meaning into their brand. Unlike Company A, Company B isn't asking for a sale in this work, they're proving why those customers should care about the brand.

After the first quarter of this activity, let's say Company A got a spike that took them from a baseline of three in sales to an activated promotional spike of seven. Every quarter thereafter, it's pretty much the same. Three to seven, and back to three. Spend again and back to seven and eventually back down to three. It's a predictable ROI, but also an expensive model without any lasting growth.

Company B has taken a longer view of the business. But, because this decreases the amount of dollars available to spend on sales activation short term, their first result on sales activation is not quite as positive as that of Company A. They go from a baseline of three to a spike of just five instead of seven.

The next quarter begins to play out the same. But then, something starts to happen.

Because Company B's brand is becoming more meaningful, their activation spend drives a higher sales peak with each successive promotional period. Customers recognize and have appreciation for the brand. The logo people see on Company B's promotional work is positively recognized and has resonance. This results in less indifference to the promotional messaging because it's from a known and appreciated brand.

The next measured quarter, Company *A* still has their jump to seven and back. However, Company *B* has now jumped to six. Next quarter a jump to seven, with a lesser activation spend than Company *A*. And something else is happening. When their activation spend ends, Company *B* is not dropping back to three — they're dropping, but to a new higher baseline of perhaps, four.

After four quarters, Company *B* has spent the same amount of money as Company *A* but allocated it differently. And now the ROI on their activation is paying off with better staying power and results that are going higher every quarter than a mere activation spend could generate. And they're not sinking back to where they were before they started the latest activation campaign.

In ensuing quarters, you can reasonably predict, Company *A* is locked in a three-to-seven then back-to-three shuffle. However, Company *B* has an activation spike that climbs higher because the number of people who recognize and appreciate the brand is growing. Even better for Company *B*, their profit margins are growing because their customers are more loyal, more appreciative, and are, therefore, less price sensitive. Company *A* will need to allocate the same budget to achieve the same results next year. Company *B* now has a sales baseline that indicates they haven't just sold more, they've taken market share.

So...CEOs. Which brand would you rather be?

Effectiveness Stacking

As marketers, we need to remember that brand and performance marketing are complementary. Too much of one, or too little, hurts our total marketing performance.

If we take Binet and Field's graph depicting the up/down of promotional spend versus the steady rise of branding and play it out over a longer term, we can put into effect something I call **Effectiveness Stacking**. That is, every time you spend money to build brand meaning, your promotional spend breaks through more easily due to a values connection you've established. More people recognize you, and more people appreciate what you stand for. This gives your promotional messaging a **Values Channel** with less clutter to cut through. Your promotional spend has more willing receivers.

Thus, as Binet and Field's research proved, the promotional spend has an ever-greater impact as your brand meaning grows.

There is no greater example of **Effectiveness Stacking** than the long-term results Dove garnered from their *Campaign for Real Beauty.*

Imagine if, at the end of the first quarter after this campaign launched, initial sales resulted in a total cancellation of this idea in favor of more promotional advertising. Would Dove have grown, as it did, from a $2.5B brand to the $4B brand in ten years? Would it have kept growing? A quick Google search says Dove in 2023 has grown to be a $6.5 billion brand.

Speaking of long-term impact, as I submit this book for publication, Dove's *Campaign for Real Beauty* keeps paying off.

The brand team recently partnered with Kylie Kelce, wife of star Philadelphia Eagles center Jason Kelce, for a sports related effort they call #keepherconfident. New research co-commissioned by Dove found 45% of girls drop out of sports by age 14 due to low body confidence. Dove is now using their brand platform to earn goodwill and appreciation for parents of young girls everywhere.

Additionally, they've just jumped into the Artificial Intelligence conversation (or controversy). It seems even AI, when prompted to: "/imagine the most beautiful woman in the world" generates the expected perfectly proportioned blonde haired blue-eyed beach beauty. But when prompted: "/imagine the most beautiful woman in the world according to Dove Real Beauty ad" a more authentic, more real, more realistically proportioned woman is generated.

Dove ends this short film with the promise that they will never use AI to distort women's images and the hashtag #keepbeautyreal.

As Dove has proven, finding that bigger problem to help solve and champion benefits the brand and the world both short term and long term.

But even small, seemingly short-term efforts can have big impact when they ring that "shared values" bell. Lacoste brand Izod case proves as much in the next chapter.

CHAPTER 7

Brands and Revenue

In a *Harvard Business Review* article, "If Brands Are Built over Years, Why Are They Managed Over Quarters," Leonard Lodish and Carl Mela share this story. After the LaCoste brand had been bought and sold, it was returned to its original owner.

> The company limited distribution to higher-quality clothing retailers, advertised the brand through celebrities, and raised prices. A change in senior leadership in 2002 precipitated an even stronger brand focus. Since that time, sales have jumped 800%. However, in the initial years after Lacoste repurchased the brand, the company's marketing efforts had little immediate effect on revenues. Had the company assumed a short-term sales perspective, it may not have been able to reinvigorate the brand.

Mounting evidence suggests that this kind of short-term orientation erodes a brand's ability to compete in the marketplace in an enduring way.

CASE STUDY: Izod Lacoste

During Paris Fashion Week in 2018, according to *USA Today*, Lacoste's "decision to produce a lineup of limited-edition

[Izod] polo shirts that replaced its iconic crocodile logo with the images of ten endangered species was a hit."

The number of shirts produced corresponded to the remaining population of each endangered species in the wild. A total of 1,175 shirts were sold representing rare reptiles, birds, and mammals.

Obviously, the goal of making these shirts was not to make transactional money. Rather, with this effort, Izod gave people a way to *live their values*. When offered, consumers gladly take that opportunity. And they appreciate you for providing it to them. Even better, they'll talk about it to someone who may become your next customer.

In this case, the surrounding word of mouth and PR for Izod amounted to millions in media impressions; impressions that were deeper and more meaningful than a TV commercial saying *"At Izod, we care about animals that are in danger of extinction. Izod. Available at fine retail establishments."* Again, doing things is more impactful than talking about doing things.

And my bet is that because it was not a self-serving promotional campaign, most who either bought one of these shirts or were exposed to this effort via word of mouth, appreciated the brand more as a result. They held it in higher esteem. Each shirt allowed its wearer to tell a story.

Measure Short and Long

Technology now makes sales data immediately available which can make long-term brand management much harder. That's why it's never been more important to include measuring brand as a longer-term metric.

"We've had an explosion over the last ten to twenty years of new ways of measuring marketing effectiveness which is great, but unfortunately, it's nearly all about measuring short-term effects," says Les Binet. "The more we measure short-term effects, the more short-term we become." The more you're just looking over the hood of your car, the more you risk ending up somewhere that wasn't part of the strategy when you set out on the highway.

Brand neglect and short-term measurement are costing brands millions in uncaptured revenue. Establishing and nurturing a values connection with your target audience opens a mental channel for customers to better connect with a brand's efforts.

My belief is the 60/40 principle as outlined by Binet and Field drives higher results because people tune in to recognized values – a **Values Channel** of sorts. Recognizing values means an increased likelihood to pay attention.

This enables promotional work to break through more effectively. We all perk up when we hear something more relevant to our interests and values. We inherently care about it and want to hear about it.

Is the Unique Selling Proposition Still Unique?

> *"Focus is the number one skill of the 21st century."*
> — Cal Newport

Advertising has always been about borrowing an audience to deliver them a message. For many, that used to mean finding your unique selling proposition, or USP. The concept of the USP was created by Rosser Reeves 100 or so years ago. *The floor cleaner that makes your kitchen smell like the forest. The tabletop electric blender that works hands free. The dish soap that softens your hands while you do the dishes.*

These early differentiators were product-based and really amounted to rational product benefits. In other words, the USP required something unique about the product to promote. Rational product differences or improvements are newsworthy and can be very effective marketing messages. In the case of the bicycle, for example, assume its first competitor had "gears that make it easier to pedal."

When rational product attributes are inevitably duplicated by a competitor, the need to find a new way to solve a customer problem that isn't so much about the product arises. That's when branding starts to really matter. The emotional associations with your brand can't be easily duplicated by another brand.

CHAPTER 8

The Brand Appreciation Pyramid

For years, what a company would *say* about its product's features and benefits is what established brand meaning. It was one-way messaging driven by what the product or service was known for solving.

Today, messaging isn't just one-way. What you *say* is only one facet of how brands must present themselves to the market.

Say, Do, Solve.

Building a brand today requires attention to three areas. Appreciation can be earned from marketing efforts in each. I've put them into what I call the **Brand Appreciation Pyramid**.

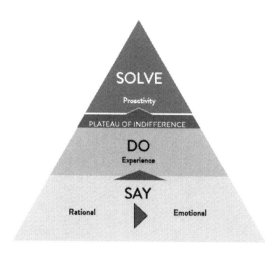

The Brand Appreciation Pyramid

SAY: At the left of the *say* zone is Rational messaging. These are the logical, rational features and benefits you say about your product or service. When a product or service is new (e.g., the bicycle) it will garner attention on its own merits. Mere explanation of a rational USP (Unique Selling Proposition) gets it noticed and cared about.

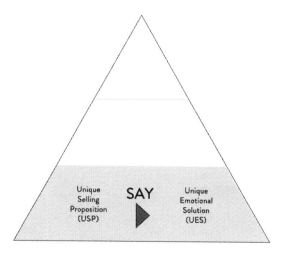

Today, Apple's products are a good example of the bottom left of the pyramid. Where rational USP appeals work because what they're saying is inherently interesting and motivating, even though they're rational appeals. The Apple Watch. AirPods. The iPad. These products solve new, yet unsolved problems. (Of course, as savvy marketers, Apple advertises them with unique voice and style. But what they're *saying* is inherently rational.)

When products get competitors in their category, the left bottom of the pyramid starts to get crowded. USP rational messaging, as "unique" as it may be thought to be by the advertiser, becomes the noise of the category. It is expected and "me-too" and is therefore much easier to ignore. The racket becomes too much for consumers to parse through as competitors try to get heard with similar features and benefits.

So, to get heard and cared about, what you *say* needs to shift from the left bottom of the Pyramid (rational) to the right side of the Pyramid (emotional). You need to find a unique emotional insight your brand gets to own.

Even today, in this cluttered media landscape, many companies believe if they just rearrange or reemphasize rational product benefits, somehow, they'll break through. But when the rational arguments for a product are no longer unique, continuing to talk about them, in any order, is an expensive, crowded path.

The marketing machete you need to cut through is something I call the **Unique Emotional Solution.** You must present your brand in a way that creates *emotional* utility or relevance. A new, unique solution based on an emotional need gives people a more meaningful reason to care about your offering over your competitors. Bonus, emotional platforms are impossible to "me-too."

A great example is the lauded and often-cited Snickers campaign from agency BBDO.

Snickers realized their "chocolatey, peanutty, nougat-y" rational ingredient message was not breaking through. And their venerable "packed with peanuts, Snickers really satisfies" message was still rational and no longer breaking through. Indulgence was the promise of the category, after all. Snickers needed to bring an emotional benefit to the table. One that would be new, universally recognizable and appreciated.

Not easy.

But they found an insight and they took ownership of it. "You're not yourself when you're hungry." This bottom right emotional appeal is a good example of the **Unique Emotional Solution.**

Suddenly, the benefit of the product isn't that it's a self-indulgent treat – the category message – it's solving a new, previously unrecognized but easily relatable problem. *You don't perform at your best when you're hungry.* So true. Thank you, Snickers.

With a **Unique Emotional Solution,** no expensive product enhancement or change was needed. Changing how the product could be appreciated made all the difference in the world. Literally. This is a global campaign that's run for years now.

APPRECIATED BRANDING

An idea like this shifted the narrative for Snickers lovers from appearing self-indulgent when they tear one open, to wanting to keep functioning at their best.

Another recent example is what agency Mischief USA did for drink pouch brand Capri Sun. Would yet another "all the flavors' kids love" rational message (at the bottom left of the Pyramid) really be something moms would appreciate?

Or would it just repeat what was already known and add to the noise? Like Snickers they realized they could make a bigger impact by uncovering a different emotional pain point.

Their **Unique Emotional Solution** for Capri Sun was "kid noise-canceling technology." Each pouch of Capri Sun gives parents "50 seconds of calm." Thank you, Capri Sun.

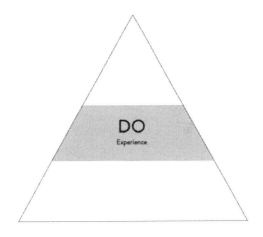

DO: Since the advent of social media, the number of places to advertise has grown and so has the clutter and noise. Marketers can make a more impactful impression by *doing* things to earn appreciation. These acts then make more impact, they're sharable and they can turn your customers into messengers for you.

Creating experiences worthy of appreciation inspire word-of-mouth, which is on steroids now with social media.

The Lexus Courtside Club at NBA games, where showing your Lexus key fob gets you into an exclusive food experience before the game, is a great example. Or creating extreme sports events, as Red Bull did to the widespread appreciation of younger consumers who wanted their love of extreme sport legitimized, organized, and celebrated.

Fixing bad customer experience is also one of a company's best opportunities to *do*.

A friend who had taken a job at the popular Midwest grocery chain recently told me about how they turned a mistake into a customer service opportunity. Hy-Vee was an innovator in the fulfillment of remote grocery orders. But when an elderly woman showed up at the prescribed time to pick up her groceries, the order hadn't been shopped yet.

The experience she ended up having included getting her groceries that day for free, a one-hundred dollar gift card for her trouble, and her next grocery order delivered free. This proactive and exceptional service gave her a story she likely went on to tell friends, family and anyone else who'd listen. Hy-Vee will make back their investment to correct their mistake many times over.

APPRECIATED BRANDING

Brands that care – and *do* something to prove it – earn appreciation and gratitude for those efforts. Those who heard her story likely shared it with others. Some even on social media.

Offering a rewards/loyalty program will earn appreciation as well. Personalization can earn appreciation, so long as it's not creepy. Surprise perks can earn appreciation, as will product sampling, demos, and exclusive offers.

Finding things for your brand to *do* creates new things for you and your customers to *say.* And it bears repeating, it is better to engage customers and inspire them to talk about your product than to highlight things only marketers care about.

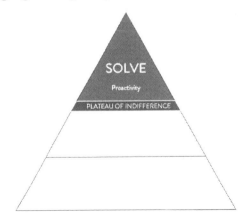

SOLVE: A brand is in the *solve* zone when it proactively helps to solve bigger issues that are related to, but not delivered by, the product that launched the brand.

Solving requires the brand to find issues or missions that are aligned with customers' values and then proactively use the brand's voice to fix or support those issues or missions.

Ariel's *#ShareTheLoad* campaign, mentioned in the introduction and featured in chapter 10, is a wonderful example of a brand that identified a problem and used its voice to help. This, and other included cases, exemplify the power of *solving*.

Additionally, *solving* includes big cost advantages because you don't have to spend years and millions in research and development, re-tool a factory, or discount your product to get attention only to end up eroding your long-term profitability.

Brands can help solve bigger problems. The smart ones will, earning them enduring appreciation, an increase in the performance of their activation marketing, and higher profitability. It also helps make the world a better place. Win. Win. Win.

CHAPTER 9

The Plateau of Indifference

The Plateau of Indifference is *the mental place consumers put brands when they know about them but there are many competing options to choose from, so they don't care which option they buy and are more influenced by price than brand.*

Self-Inflicted Brand Purgatory

Influence doesn't increase because you say something at higher volume, or more often, or in a "harder hitting" way.

If your brand is stagnant, and all you ever do is talk about yourself, your brand is on the **Plateau of Indifference.** People have your number; they just don't want to call it.

There's an inflection point in a business's growth where the novelty and newness of the product has worn off.

Peter Field said, "It's hard to generalize, but the first time a small to medium-sized business should think about branding on a larger scale is when they can no longer kid themselves that they're the new kid on the block. Their technology has been copied, perhaps their unique panache or sense of self as a brand is no longer as exciting as it once was. At that point, they're going to cease to benefit from the 'new' and they'll have to start to create something of their own to take them forward."

It's not enough to talk louder, or re-organize your USP, you must shatter consumers' habits and patterns around a brand so they stop taking you for granted. This is where proactive proof that you care about them in bigger ways gets you off the **Plateau of Indifference** to earning new growth.

In the movie *The Blues Brothers,* after Jake arrives at Elwood's little shoebox Chicago apartment, he notices the elevated train track right outside the window. A train passes making such a ruckus that Jake asks Elwood, "So how often does the train come by?" Elwood replies, "So often you won't even notice it."

The repetition of rational category benefits garners a similar response in marketing. It won't get your customers' attention nor get them off the **Plateau of Indifference,** where they habitually tune you out like a noisy El train.

Could there be a more obvious indicator of the **Plateau of Indifference** than an entire grocery aisle offering some thirty different laundry detergent brands? That's over fifty years of rational product appeals and marginal product improvements, all stacked on shelves eight feet high and thirty feet long. Each brand couponing, discounting, blasting "whiter whites" or "brighter colors" messaging, and all creating essentially the same outcome.

Many brands, especially mature ones, are on the Plateau and may not even know it. They spend millions on promotional advertising and earn meager share growth, only to lose it the next quarter when their competitor does the same thing. It feeds right into the short-term mindset, resulting in what I call the **Share Shuffle.** A spending race to nowheresville.

That's why you need to own the true meaning behind your brand and prove it. Foster, feed, and champion the values you and your customers share by finding bigger problems to proactively *solve*.

Getting Off The Plateau of Indifference

Customers are more apt to *believe in the brand that believes in them.*

Identify a problem your customers would appreciate having fixed. Become the voice that empathetically says, in essence, we know you really care about this. We see it, too, and we want to help.

Now you have a shot at getting attention, making a positive impression, and getting off the **Plateau of Indifference.** Help make your customer's experience better, and you gain attention, influence, and growth.

What can your brand do to help solve a problem your customers will appreciate? Is there a constituency of people in your target market that believe in something strongly that your brand can authentically support? Are there any data points that support an effort to fix something?

I once was asked to help my agency pitch the Mayo Clinic advertising account. They wanted to "increase appointment generation." The stature of the Mayo Clinic brand is such that I didn't think it was right to do TV commercials with an 800 number at the end. Our astute and relentless account planner,

Lynn Franz, found a data point that immediately jumped off the page. "97% of former Mayo patients wanted to tell others about the amazing experience."

Out of that insight came an idea we called Mayo Mentors. We proposed a "Facebook for health" website that allowed anyone to get tips, advice, and guidance from a former Mayo patient. What insurance do they take? Do I have to be a Saudi prince or a rock star to get care there? What if I have a non-life threatening but kinda complex issue, would they help with that? Empowering former patients to speak on behalf of the brand not only helped increase appointments, but it has also since become a tool that improves patient outcomes. (You can find it online today under the name: Mayoclinic.com/connect.) And yours truly was interviewed by The New York Times because it was so innovative.

What new or missed data points are there that might inspire your brand to take action to solve a different, unaddressed problem? What disadvantages are our customers facing in the marketplace that you can proactively help them with? What can your brand do that will be *useful*?

With media as splintered as ever, the opportunity to target people based on the values they share with your brand has never been more possible, or necessary. When your appeal is based on human values, you have that existing open **Values Channel** your customers are already tuned in to. You just need to fill it with something your brand can add value to. Ignoring those opportunities can cost you the chance to spark an entirely new era of growth for your brand.

Re-inspire Lapsed Brand Lovers

Most marketers have been focusing on *saying* and *doing* for decades. But they're using old tools to achieve marginal results. With a **Unique Emotional Solution**, brands are more noticeable. And the clear emotional benefit that it reveals will help inform the things you can *do* and *solve*.

Solving is the root of every success I cite in this book. Below is the full Appreciation Pyramid for reference.

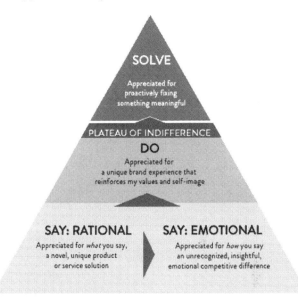

Groundhog Day

The iconic movie *Groundhog Day* is a great example of how to get off the **Plateau of Indifference**.

Phil Connors (Bill Murray) is the embodiment of thousands of brands who think they're important, irresistible, and that people care about them.

Phil is interested in his coworker Rita, (Andie MacDowell) but she's already told him, "I could never love someone like you. You only love yourself."

Rita has Phil on the **Plateau of Indifference.**

As the movie progresses, Phil starts to finally understand that his selfish efforts to win Rita over are not going to work. Thanks to the repeating of Groundhog Day, he gets to know Rita's human side. He starts to understand her motivations, beliefs, and values.

He starts to realize that, to win someone over, you must make it about them, not you.

Phil makes a proactive effort to earn Rita's attention, and she starts to see him in a different light. The positive and proactive energy coming from Phil caused her to reconsider.

She stopped being indifferent to him. And because he clearly started to care about her, she started to care about him.

CHAPTER 10

The Expected and The Appreciated

What a brand says, does and solves can be either rational, or emotional. The rational, for products that aren't unique and noteworthy on their own, is expected. Easy to duplicate for competitors and easy to ignore for customers.

The emotional, when a brand has found a **Unique Emotional Solution**, tends to break through, earn deeper appreciation, and offer a platform to solve bigger problems. For illustrative purposes, I've added these to each side of the Pyramid.

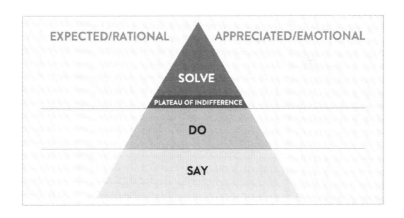

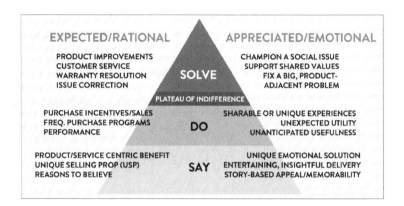

Starting from the bottom left, I've outlined what each section usually contains. From the lower left, *saying* your rational USP, to *doing* things that try to earn allegiance, and finally to *solving* things related to the rational use of the product. I call this the "expected" side because these are the things customers simply expect from brands today.

Moving to the bottom right, the emotional side of *saying*. This is where, for example, a **Unique Emotional Solution** like Snickers' "you're not yourself when you're hungry" lives. It allows for the brand to *say* in a much more emotional, interesting, differentiated way. When your brand is defined by such an insightful and unique emotional platform, the emotional things you *do* then become much clearer.

As an example, Snickers in the UK enlisted five celebrities and Twitter (at the time) to do the doing for the brand. Each celebrity sent four out-of-character tweets, before revealing in a fifth tweet that they had been hungry and needed a Snickers. As an example of the power of *doing* to earn attention, national newspapers picked up the story and it reached more than 26 million people.

APPRECIATED BRANDING

Moving up the right side, what you *solve*. In the case of Snickers, what they solved was based on their **Unique Emotional Solution**. But they got very specific. They leveraged their iconic package design and typeface by replacing the word Snickers with words like "loopy," "snippy," "grouchy," "sleepy," "rebellious," and even "impatient." You could choose the one that best represented the emotional problem you needed solved in that moment.

The Black Hole of Opportunity

The upper right side of the pyramid is where your best opportunities exist to get new growth for your mature brand by getting it off the **Plateau of Indifference**.

Solving an emotionally based problem proactively for your customers – or those you want to be your customers – is a wide-open space. The is a huge opportunity that will earn attention, be appreciated, and create enduring loyalty.

Here's the Pyramid of Appreciation for the Dove case study featured in chapter 6.

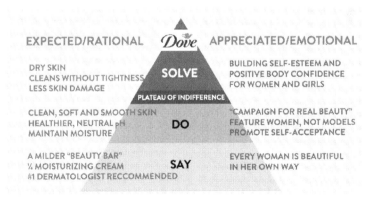

SECTION 3

WHY SHOULD PEOPLE CARE?

CHAPTER 11

The Heart of Appreciated Branding - Caring

People connect with what they care about and value. They won't care about you unless they've sensed that *you* care about *them*. It's human nature. That means solving problems for them that earns their attention and appreciation.

This is why, at the heart of every successful campaign is a thank you, whether consciously acknowledged, or not. A laugh is a thank you. A new solution is a thank you. A joyful response is a thank you. A new piece of information earns a thank you. A reinforcing of someone's beliefs and values earns a thank you. Solving a problem earns a thank you. An insight that evokes a "I hadn't thought about it that way before" earns a thank you. Something useful that allows people to be better earns a thank you.

Of course, the biggest thank you is in the "debt of gratitude." People want what you sell more than the money it takes to get it. Cash, in that sense, is the original thank you note.

The most famous quote by Howard Gossage is more relevant than ever: "People don't read ads, they read what interests them. And sometimes, that's an ad."

People are busier than ever. It's getting harder for people who are naturally in the middle of doing something else to care about giving attention to your ad. We humans care about ourselves first. That's the prime directive. Put your mask on before assisting others. Whatever is out there that is going to help us, that's what we most immediately care about.

Appreciated Brands show an *understanding* for the problems humans face every day and take action to help proactively fix those problems. Brands that do this earn better results, have more impact, and market endurance.

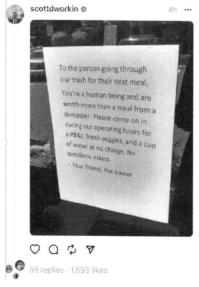

A poster meant for an audience of one yet imagine how the business earned interest and appreciation from such a kind, proactive gesture.

APPRECIATED BRANDING

A screen grab from an appreciative passenger's posted video. Southwest Airlines has a tradition of singing Happy Birthday to their customers. After the song, the flight attendant asks everyone to "blow out those candles" and everyone turns out their call light. This photo, found on social media, is essentially customer-placed, story-based branding.

> *"Ahh. What a joy to be understood."*
> — Abraham Lincoln, as played by Daniel Day-Lewis in the movie Lincoln.

Harvesting Requires Planting

Marketing has become focused on sales harvesting. But long before the harvest, you must first plant the seeds. That, essentially, is what branding does. That's what gives people reason to listen to you, pay attention and care about what you're trying to say. It's that top of the purchase funnel stuff that feeds the action part at the bottom.

Your Customers Should be Your Best Influencers

Customers who don't just buy what you sell but feel like you care will hold you in higher esteem. And, in that sense, energized, vocal customers can become an "earned media" channel unto themselves via their social followings. Appreciative customers are the most authentic voice a brand has for a commodity product to differentiate itself in this new marketing landscape. You must inspire the people you sell to, so they then give energy back by attracting others to the brand.

Customer Service: The Front Line of Branding

This is a deep cut, but still a great example of how an indifferent company can draw attention. In 2008, a Canadian musician watched in horror as United Airlines' baggage handlers threw his guitar onto a plane like it was a side of beef. When nobody at the airline seemed to care about his damaged guitar, he wrote a song about it. And then he posted it on YouTube.

"United Breaks Guitars" was among the first customer-generated content to go viral.

Keep in mind, this wasn't even a marketing blunder. It was merely an event witnessed by a dumbfounded customer who used social media to share his experience.

And it was a huge opportunity missed by a marketer at the time who, like most, was still coming to terms with the fact that brands don't drive the conversation anymore.

United could have used this negative attention to respond proactively, positively, and generously. Imagine the

APPRECIATED BRANDING

appreciation they'd have earned if they'd bought him a new guitar or offered him free flights, or both?

When a brand knows what a customer cares deeply about, in this case a cherished guitar, it has an emotional channel through which to earn appreciation. Not taking advantage of it, or merely ignoring it, is a missed opportunity.

CASE STUDY: Ariel Detergent, India

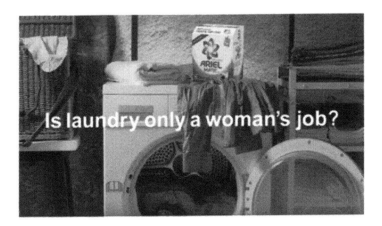

Ariel, removing the stains of gender inequality has managed to build a social property, #ShareTheLoad and brought in an amalgamation of their brand identity and an ideology of their belief, thus crafting an initiative that sprints beyond just social media marketing.

Proctor & Gamble's (P&G) Ariel brand laundry detergent in India was in a constant share battle with Surf, a Unilever brand. Year after year, they each played this **Share Shuffle**, two different brands competing for market share by alternately spending their promotional budgets and to steal share from one another. An arms race, of sorts. Each spent millons on typical category "whiter whites" or "brighter colors" messaging, with pretty much no lasting impact.

P&G decided to make a more emotional appeal based on a unique cultural/societal data point. As a company in the laundry category, it was a problem they were credibly positioned to help fix: *In 95% of households in India, only women did the laundry.*

Ariel's smart marketing agency team recognized this was a societal, gender-based tension upon which to prove how their values overlap with those of their main purchasers, moms. Ariel realized they could use their brand's voice to champion a solution, and, in so doing, earn the appreciation of millions of their most important customers.[14]

The brand became a vocal advocate for everyone in the family to #ShareTheLoad. In commercials they depicted mom coming home from work, starting dinner, picking up clutter, taking work calls, all while dad rests on the couch reading the evening paper and her teenage son shouts from upstairs that he needs his green shirt washed.

She keeps moving, doing all she has to do since getting home. She puts a load of clothes in the washer, picks up toys from the floor, and gets back to preparing dinner for everyone. It's

---

[14] Richa Tallreja, "Ariel Share the Load Case Film," June 16, 2017, YouTube video, 1:29, https://www.youtube.com/watch?v=sFDfcV-efng.

APPRECIATED BRANDING

a familiar scene, not just in India. By calling attention to an unrecognized problem and advocating for it to change, Ariel was rewarded with a result that few "buy now" performance marketing campaigns could ever achieve. *In its first year the campaign drove a 76% increase in sales.*[24]

#ShareTheLoad has shown no signs of slowing down. Since its launch in 2015, the brand has been number one in India. That kind of success doesn't come from talking about your formula or your efficacy, it comes from an empathetic understanding of your customers' lives and proactively helping to solve their problems.

#ShareTheLoad gave millions of current customers and potential new customers an opening to think about how society could change for the better.

The 1+1=3 power of leveraging overlapping company and customer values to drive massive sales gains and share is undeniable. Competing for share in a mature category like laundry detergent using performance marketing alone has always been expensive and usually delivered marginal gains.

Ariel uncovered an opportunity for the brand to earn gratitude from millions of women who wanted help. What I love about this campaign is that it wasn't just about purpose, or some kind of altruistic mission. Advocating for this mission on behalf of customers was a powder keg of growth just waiting to explode. And importantly, it was a powder keg only for the brand that found it and had the courage to use it. Prominent women like Sheryl Sandberg and Melinda Gates pointed out *#ShareTheLoad* on social platforms. The campaign had a shared viewership of over 65 million people across twenty-two countries.

Ariel took their messaging further, and some would say did some non-traditional things. They introduced men's laundry packs. They incorporated alternating male/female laundry day calendars on the packaging. Ariel even partnered with garment makers who changed clothing labels to include the message "This garment is washable by men."

Here's the Brand Appreciation Pyramid as applied to the case for Ariel.

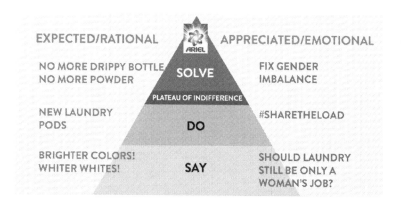

> *"Is advertising worth saving? Yes, if we can learn to look at advertising not as a means for filling so much space and time but as a technique for solving problems."*
> —Howard Gossage

The Power of Emotional Recognition

When you realize someone understands your values and beliefs, it sparks emotional energy. Different neurons fire. Perhaps a smile spreads across your face. It's a kind of **Emotional Recognition**; a recognized visual cue creates an involuntary emotional response. Like seeing someone you know across the room at a party, it gets your focus, your recognition.

Same thing holds true for a logo that gets recognized. It is either appreciated or ignored.

Mature brands already have a head start because they are a recognized and known quantity. The rational problems you solve are known and you already get credit for them.

To earn new attention, you need a new story.

To find those stories, look at the values you share, make sure they are relevant and resonate with your company and your customers, and act on them. Older brands can take advantage of opportunities to stand for something that will be appreciated and consequently inspire new attention, and greater brand loyalty.

Rational Appeals Get Rations. Emotional Appeals Get Motion.

A compelling illustration of this is a powerful short video that's been done in a few variations and is easily located on YouTube. A man sits on a blanket in a park next to a walking path. He has a tin can sitting out and a cardboard sign that says, "Blind. Please help." Folks walk by, but he's getting little charity. His cup remains empty. After a while, a young woman happens by, stops, turns around, and returns to do something for him.

As he feels her shoes to try to identify just who this might be, she picks up his sign and writes something on the other side of it. It's not clear to us what she writes. But she displays the new sign without telling him what she wrote and continues on her way.

Now, when people see the sign, coins drop from almost every passerby. After a much more productive afternoon, the man excitedly gathers the coins into his tin can to wrap up his day. The young lady who had changed the message on his sign returns on her way back home.

She stops and the blind man recognizes her by the feel of her shoes. "What did you do to my sign?" he asked. "I just wrote the same thing, only different." At this point, we are finally shown what she wrote: "It's a beautiful day, and I can't see it."

Just by turning the message around from being about him, to being about something emotionally recognizable to everyone made all the difference to get attention and inspire action.

CASE STUDY: Ruavieja

Liqueur is a product category so crowded with brands it's impossible to fit them all behind one decent-sized bar.

Spanish crème liqueur brand Ruavieja realized in 2018 that if they were going to stand out from the hundreds of bottles behind that bar, they needed to create a better reason to get people to care about their brand.

The powerful insight they discovered wasn't about their brand specifically, it was about the role liqueur can play in people's lives; a time to slow down, talk, and enjoy each other's company.

Using data from the Spanish National Institute of Statistics, Ruavieja developed an online calculator so people could figure out the real amount of time the subjects of the experiment would have together before they died. Where most believed it was the rest of their lives – decades – the data revealed that after accounting for the usual day to day activities, responsibilities and distractions of life, the time we have left to spend with loved ones is not years, months, or weeks, it's closer to mere days and hours.

When Ruavieja then brought together great friends or family and asked for their reaction to this news, people in this video are visibly moved. And their appreciation for this important revelation and for the brand is undeniable.

Ruavieja's *"We have to see more of each other"* became the most watched and shared Spanish ad in history. Sales went up 52%.

"We are programmed to avoid thinking how long we have left to live. So, we think we'll always have time to do the things that really make us happy," says psychologist Rafael Santandreu about the campaign.

This is a great example of the higher purpose that can be accomplished by brand action. Using non-commoditized thinking to help sell a commodity in a way people will forever appreciate.

EXPECTED/RATIONAL	Ruavieja	APPRECIATED/EMOTIONAL
RUAVIEJA LIGHT LACTOSE FREE & VEGAN	**SOLVE**	TIME WITH LOVED ONES
MULTIPLE FLAVORS LIMITED "RICE" CREAM NEW PACKAGING!	PLATEAU OF INDIFFERENCE **DO**	THE "TIME WE HAVE LEFT" CALCULATOR
FULL OF FLAVOR RELAX AFTER DINNER SINCE 1889	**SAY**	CONSCIOUS LIFE ENJOYMENT

CHAPTER 12

The Importance of Story

> *"Storytelling will be over when the world is perfect. I don't think we're there yet."*
>
> –Susan Credle, Global Creative Advisor, IPG, first ever woman to be named Chair of the One Club for Creativity

There's a reason people say, "Hey, remember that time…" and they never say, "Hey, remember that information about…"

Stories are easier to take in and remember. It's just data with table stakes, tension, and winners and losers.

Stories Get Remembered. Data Points Get Forgotten.

Stories involve an emotional connection. Stories give information memorable context. Stories develop and advance to a conclusion. Stories hold interest. Data points are static.

Notice how on the left of the Brand Appreciation Pyramid, the expected benefits of *saying, doing,* and *solving* can leave you wondering if the same benefits could be found cheaper somewhere else?

On the right, you've been lifted out of the rational benefit, price mentality. You're in a story now. You get to be a part of it.

The Significant Objects Project

A real-world example of the power of story is The Significant Objects Project, an experiment from early 2009. The project and the titular book detail the findings of Rob Walker and Joshua Glenn.

These two men searched junk stores and flea markets in New York City and bought one hundred items – mostly novelty items, plastic toys, and trinkets. These were not unusual or special or expensive items. They spent a total of just $129.

As part of the experiment, they created a compelling story about each item to accompany its listing on eBay.

One of my favorites was about an object that appeared to have about 15 metal rods sewn into a square piece of fabric. The story that was created referred to this thing as a "Voice Crumpter." Allegedly, back in the '50s, you would use the "Crumpter" to encircle the microphone and it would ensure your voice would be recorded in perfect pitch.

In his article, "The Experiment That Proves the Value of Stories," Keith Browning, Director, Brand Marketing at Linked In, explains,

"Walker and Glenn's idea was that the emotional value that comes from attaching a story to an everyday object is so strong that it can be measured in terms of objective, actual value."

What the buyer is now buying isn't just an inanimate object, it's a significant item with an interesting history.

After spending $129 on the objects, they sold the items with accompanying stories for $3,612.51.

Stories pay off.

Recognize an Emotional Problem You Can Help Solve

"Who wants to sign up for my tennis lessons?" is certainly one way to pitch your tennis coaching business to attract clients. But it's not very compelling. It doesn't identify a specific differentiating value proposition. So, it's no wonder this tennis coach wasn't getting any new students to sign up.

A mentor and sales coach of mine, Steve Lowell, recognized that a message that doesn't identify a bigger solution is doomed to be ignored. Steve suggested the tennis pro find a specific, recognizable problem tennis lessons can solve.

He changed the sales pitch to: "Who has kids bouncing off the walls?" That message gets mental gears turning. Suddenly, it's not about selling tennis lessons, it's about solving a bigger problem for people; providing kids with a positive activity, getting them moving, and introducing them to a sport they might enjoy for life. All while solving a different problem for parents, giving them some peace and quiet.

Reframing the problem your product solves is one of the keys to creating differentiation, earning attention, and inspiring appreciation.

Punxsutawney – The Point

Seeing through the eyes of your customer is critical. Back to the movie *Groundhog Day*. Phil Connors transformed from being completely absorbed with himself and his needs alone into someone who understands the power of sincerity, connection, and proactive problem solving.

At the evening dance and bachelor auction, Rita showers Phil with gratitude and joy, "This day was perfect. You couldn't have planned a day like this."

"Well, you can," Phil says. "It just takes some work."

This first new day after Groundhog Day, Phil's transformation is obvious. He even asks Rita, "Is there anything I can do for you today?"

This is the approach branding must take if we want it to live up to its potential.

APPRECIATED BRANDING

CASE STUDY: Deluxe

Robert Herjavec, entrepreneurial expert, and Amanda Brinkman, former Chief Brand and Content Officer at Deluxe.[15]

In 2014, Deluxe Corporation was known as a check printing company. Not a good place to be given the global shift to digital payments. Checks were quickly going the way of the bowler hat. In fact, the younger you were, the less you knew about them.

Deluxe was essentially spending millions on promotional marketing – a fraction of what their competitors were spending – with an occasional overlay of a paid brand campaign. But it wasn't moving the needle. They were being outspent 14 to 1 by competitors like VistaPrint, Constant Contact, and GoDaddy.

People didn't have reason to care about Deluxe. The brand had incredibly low awareness and those who were aware didn't have reason to take new interest. Few even knew that the company had evolved, and they now had an entire suite of services to support small businesses and their marketing needs.

Amanda Brinkman, former Chief Brand and Content Officer at Deluxe, believes in good old fashioned customer interaction. Get out of the office and to talk to the people. Get to know their

---

[15] "Small Business Revolution," Deluxe, accessed November 2023, https://www.deluxe.com/small-business-revolution/.

issues, their challenges, and be open minded and optimistic about finding a way to help solve them.

Out of that kind of interaction came *The Small Business Revolution (SBR)*, an original, unscripted series that put Amanda and various other pros on the ground in these small towns helping small business owners to better compete and win.

This small business makeover show of sorts streamed on Hulu and was also available online at a dedicated site. The effort was so successful, it went on to run for six seasons and earned a few Emmy nominations.

I've admired this effort since I first saw it. It smartly redefined the brand and the company as proactive problem solvers. Deluxe employees even stopped Amanda in the parking lot to tell her how proud the show made them feel as part of the company.

According to the dedicated website: "The mission came out of a recognition that nowhere are small businesses more under siege than in small towns. We created the Small Business Revolution to help those small businesses, and, in turn, those small towns, reignite the spark that drives them and keeps people coming back."

This investment to rebuild relevant meaning into the Deluxe brand probably wasn't born out of a strategic intention to earn appreciation, but looking at it from the outside, one can't help but see how it did just that. It was a completely new way forward for a brand that needed to redefine and re-energize its meaning. It gave people a new reason to care.

It inspires the question at the very heart of Appreciated Branding: *"What do our customers or prospects need our help with?"*

For *SBR*, the emphasis wasn't about Deluxe *claiming* to do things differently or better, but rather about showcasing *how* Deluxe does it. Hard hit business owners didn't need, or respond, to being sold a suite of tools. What they needed in that moment was someone who cared. They needed help.

As Amanda put it to me, "We had less than 1% brand awareness among small businesses, not to mention the hurricane competitive spend we found ourselves in. With this campaign, we needed to do something completely different than our competitors to stand out. Instead of being just another company that sold to them – could we be their advocates, be seen as their champions and stand by them? To truly do something GOOD for them?"

By season four, Deluxe had garnered 5.7 billion media impressions from more than 3,600 news stories, an achievement that would have been impossible using traditional interruptive media, especially when the Deluxe budget was a fraction of their competitors.

This case is proof of what brands can do to give people a reason to care. Proactively helping those they want as customers and helping make them better at running their small businesses, paid off. And the video content gave other business owners a peek into how they could improve their game. Really smart.

The series put small businesses at the center of focus, not the Deluxe brand. Any viewer will understand the Deluxe role without having to put the brand in their face. The brand took action to prove that they're on their customers' side in the fight, helping to make them and their businesses better versions of themselves. That is the key. "It can't just be a show," said Amanda, "it has to be real."

Research by the Content Marketing Institute further proves the impact of this type of work. According to Aberdeen Group, a Boston-based research firm, content that doesn't explicitly promote a brand costs 62% less than more traditional outbound marketing and generates three times as many leads. Why? Because viewers can sense when it's about them, not you.

Amanda lives by the wonderful mantra: *Do well by doing good*. By finding a way to genuinely help people, brands can communicate with their customers on that mental channel they already tune into. It's about *you* proving you understand their problems and how you can help.

Some see this as wasting valuable marketing dollars because they're not considered hardworking or measurable. But "above the line" promotion investment doesn't drive brand allegiance. C-Suites may like the measurability, but constant interruption in our lives is becoming so intrusive and unwelcome, it's ignored at scale. It's mostly seen as ad pollution.

With the *SBR* series and corresponding press coverage around it, Deluxe reached 14X more people than a traditional paid ad campaign would have. They confirmed what Binet and Field's advertising research proved, that a brand that seeks to create more meaning will experience higher performance from their activation marketing.

Brands today are expected to, and can do, so much more proactive good that earns appreciation and translates to profit. And when they do, every other marketing tactic they employ has more meaning and impact. Deluxe effectively found a way to put their customers' needs first, and in so doing, get far more attention.

APPRECIATED BRANDING

Congratulations to Amanda and the entire Deluxe team. They did good. For the Deluxe business. For their customers. For small towns. And for themselves.

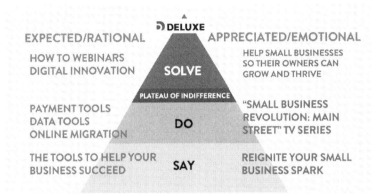

SECTION 4

PUTTING APPRECIATED BRANDING INTO PRACTICE

CHAPTER 13

Building an Appreciated Brand

Being appreciated by a customer means they stay with your brand longer and buy more. According to a recent article in *Forbes*, once you establish a personal connection: "You get much more than traditional loyalty — you get a vocal, engaged advocate for your brand." Customers who care about your brand will extend your reach by word of mouth.

A personal endorsement from a current consumer, not a marketer with an agenda, is more credible and impactful. In fact, loyal customers will create more loyal customers than most any ad. And loyal customers spend ten times more with your business than new ones.[16]

Brand Appreciation forces you to approach selling and brand building from the customer's perspective – what's in it for them? Brands who, like *Groundhog Day's* Phil Connors, think that people reflexively care about them will find more and more people indifferent to their selfish appeals.

---

[16] Rob Danna, "How Emotional Connections Create Champions for Your Brand," Forbes, December 22, 2017, https://www.forbes.com/sites/forbescommunicationscouncil/2017/12/22/how-emotional-connections-create-champions-for-your-brand.

The Power of Proactivity

I recently heard this story and it couldn't be more appropriate here. A real estate agent was trying to get clients and build his business. His face and phone number were displayed on the back of bus benches and billboards, but he wasn't getting traction.

One day, he learned of a garbage strike going on in the area, the very community where he was trying to build up his client base.

After weeks of garbage piling up in these neighborhoods, he got an idea.

He took some of his non-performing ad budget and hired a garbage company. The folks in the neighborhood got home to find their bins empty and thought "finally, the strike is over." Wisely, this agent stayed quiet and didn't actively take credit for his generous act.

Inevitably, word got out. One after one, homeowners called the agent and wanted to reimburse him for their share of the cost. He told them there's no need, but if they ever want to sell their house, or know someone looking to buy in the area, to send them his way.

Within a year, this agent made over a million dollars in commissions. His proactive effort to do some good for his targeted clientele earned their appreciation and their business. His efforts got attention, he was off the **Plateau of Indifference** and had become an Appreciated Brand.

This kind of proactivity builds momentum for more sustainable, defendable, exponential growth. A brand that has made an investment in solving a bigger problem for its customers earns bigger emotional interest, attention, and investigation from those customers. Why? Because you're not just hawking product, you're helping first.

A Purpose We Can All Agree On

The purpose of Brand Appreciation is to improve the daily lives of your customers and prospects in a tangible way. That can be seen as purpose-driven in the traditional sense, and in many cases, it will be. But it differs from bigger altruistic efforts because you're not just backing a purpose to improve a perception of your company, you're providing something very useful at the moment of exposure to your customers.

For example, a company might have a mission to improve the rainforest. So, they donate money to that end. An Appreciated Brand would find ways to help in a more targeted way. Like planting trees at a local park.

Brand Appreciation incorporates the need for companies to experience improved profits through a more meaningful and influential brand. Sometimes that makes a positive social impact and sometimes it just makes the brand's customers better versions of themselves. Sometimes it's both.

Either way, it solves a problem, earns attention, and drives meaningful brand and sales growth.

Finding A Human Truth

> *What happens if you get scared half to death twice?*
> — Steven Wright

In my experience, like a good joke, great advertising earns a thank you because it respects a viewer's intelligence and reveals a new and interesting insight that brand or product solves. A viewer should be thinking "that's so true." Or "I hadn't thought about it that way but … totally!"

Find something that has never been expressed but is recognizable, makes you think, and is inarguably *true*.

Renowned comedian George Carlin said one of my favorite truths of all time, "Everyone smiles in the same language."

Remember the Snickers example? "You're not yourself when you're hungry" is a human truth because it's fresh, but familiar.

Creative people in ad agencies relentlessly seek to uncover unrecognized human truths. These truths once revealed have tremendous value because they have universal appeal, resonate emotionally, and spark new synapses.

Yet because companies often think the job of their ads is to explain the rational benefits of their product, these motivating truths remain unclaimed. And results remain flat.

Human truths shift meaning from rational to emotional. From dry data to a memorable story.

Many clients discard ideas that they think aren't "ownable" or that they think "anyone can say." That's a mistake. The Snickers idea could have been used by any quick, high-energy snack like trail mix, or another candy bar, or plain old peanuts, for that matter. The human truth uncovered by the brand was a memorable way to put a high calorie/high-energy product at the center of multiple stories where the product was the hero. Had the brand decided not to use it, they would have left a huge advantage on the table for a competitor.

The best advertising appeals to values your audience already recognizes and believes in. That's how the stories connect with viewers. You aren't being sold something overtly; you're being offered help, via an insight that is very hard to argue with.

The Question is the Same. The Answer is Always Changing.

You must ask critical questions about who you are as a company. What were your founding values? What are the values that will instill pride in your workforce? Exactly what are your customers' values that your brand can champion?

It is likely the same question that was asked at your founding, but it will have a different answer today.

For example, laundry powder was created over a century ago. The question likely asked by the brand then is equally relevant today; "How can we best help our customers get their clothes clean?"

Back then, when the automatic washing machine was an emerging innovation, washing powder was the new and novel solution to get the most out of that invention. So, the answer was likely something rational: "Just one scoop cleans the whole load!"

As times change, the most powerful way to connect with your customer is evolving. The question is the same: "How can we best help our customers get their clothes clean?"

But the right answer is one that shows you understand your customers' lives and the problems they face today. The context has changed. Women have had more and more chores piled onto them over the decades since the benefit of "just one scoop cleans a whole load."

That solution is now table stakes for the category. The answer to the question went from "one scoop cleans a whole load" to "doing laundry shouldn't just be a woman's job anymore."

The Value of Proving Your Values

Brands and branded products – in mature categories in particular – have a huge opportunity to prove their values – the things they believe in – to customers who appreciate those values. The ones that do this bring energy, inspiration, and deeper levels of devotion to their brand and business.

CASE STUDY: Liquid Death

Aligning with what your customers care about can create a huge brand even when the actual product has no inherent rational difference to exploit. One great example of this is the most mature product of them all: water.

APPRECIATED BRANDING

In 2018, the Liquid Death Mountain Water brand launched under an irreverent and attention-getting name with the tagline "Murder Your Thirst." The Liquid Death brand exploded by simultaneously championing the kind of absurd entertainment younger generations appreciate, and by advocating for the aluminum can as the better, more environmentally responsible option for water.

According to Liquid Death's website, 95% of plastic water bottles end up in landfills. So, their "evil mission is to get people to laugh and to drink more healthy beverages more often, all while helping to kill plastic pollution."

By offering a variety of products (flavored and not flavored, carbonated and non), the brand fundamentally offers nothing different than many other water or canned drink brand.

But the brand's entertaining approach in what they *say* and in what they *do* to earn attention and create a unique experience makes people proud to associate with the brands. They earn appreciation from those who share the values of being entertaining, anomalous, and absurd.

Even better, by helping to proactively contribute to *solving* an environmental cause, they are further appreciated. For all those reasons, they have become an Appreciated Brand.

As Liquid Death VP, Andy Pierson, stated, "We don't spend money on media because we've prioritized making entertainment instead of marketing. We just make stuff the people genuinely want to see and interact with. And then we don't have to spend money to force people to watch it."[17]

Amen.

Clearly, people appreciate a fresh, new voice that's backed by a meaningful social mission. Remember, it's the commodity of all commodities: water. In a can.

Championing an important cause that lifts the voice of people who share those values earns appreciation. Those who want their water with a laugh chaser made Liquid Death a $700 million dollar brand by 2022. And in early 2024 its valuation doubled to $1.4 billion with a new round of investors who see nothing but growth from this commodity that is marketed as anything but.

Liquid Death built meaning into its brand by saying something about what its drinkers value. Holding a can with its creatively designed logo is a personal badge that means something worthy of the $2 per-can price tag.

To the uninitiated, it offers a sense of mystique and intrigue; and from those who get its irreverent attitude, it inspires a nod from a fellow drinker and member of the club.

---

[17] Naree Asherian, "The Water That Looks Like Beer: Liquid Death Marketing Case Study," NoGood, July 31, 2023, https://nogood.io/2023/07/31/liquid-death-marketing/.

APPRECIATED BRANDING

Liquid Death's absurd brand voice isn't for everyone. But that's the point.

Recently Liquid Death used hate comments they received on the internet to further push their brash style.[18] They set them to music, creating a series of videos, and released music CDs as a marketing effort. This stance energized the true fan base and strengthened the community of Liquid Death lovers like they were part of a tribe. Appreciation earned.

As James Gray, American film director and screenwriter, said, "If everybody loves you, you must be doing something wrong."

Critically for Liquid Death and Ariel detergent, the reason their sales exploded had no rational connection to their products' efficacy or benefits. These brands championed values that their customers' respect and live by, which gave customers and prospects a new reason to care. And in so doing, earned their appreciation.

---

[18] Liquid Death, "Liquid Death Internet Hater Comments Set to '80s Dance Songs," June 28, 2023, YouTube video, 1:05, https://www.youtube.com/watch?v=PMbpARpdgz4.

Red Bull is another example of a brand that puts its values where its brand is. They don't just *say* that they're Formula One (F1) racing fans. They don't just spend money sponsoring F1 broadcasts. They put the brand at the center of the F1 experience by outright owning and financing an F1 team. Not cheap, but hugely energizing for the brand.

Through acts like this, Red Bull has built itself into a similar badge brand for lovers of extreme sports. The logo itself has become so synonymous with extreme sports that participants take great pride in posting selfies from these events with the Red Bull logo prominently displayed. This is a great example of how doing something worth talking about results in it getting talked about by your customers.

Championing values is how brands today are meaningfully breaking through the onslaught of messaging and media that are growing every day. It's how brands are becoming a part of customers' lives.

Earning appreciation requires that a brand is standing for something bigger than the rational benefits of its product. It helps make the brand a part of people's stories. It helps people see the brand as vital, meaningful, and worth caring about.

CHAPTER 14

Getting Started

Empathetically getting into your customer's shoes and finding that emotionally differentiating thing your brand can uniquely say, do, or solve to earn appreciation is the key.

How do you get there?

Empathy

Many marketers buy a media plan first and then do the math on impressions they can get for their money. Then they fill those spaces with their message.

Starting with media is like renting Madison Square Garden and then finding out if you can book Taylor Swift or Bob's Jug Band. Ideas have a reliable way of telling you where they want to live so they can prosper and get traction. Jamming an idea into a media form isn't best for the business, the idea, or the brand.

In my view, and I know I'm not alone here, it doesn't put the interests of the brand first. Given the power of a strong brand to drive effectiveness, without an idea to guide the effort, you're robbing the business of a huge opportunity to drive growth.

Using the *Brand Appreciation Pyramid* as a guide, the idea may best end up working in *earned* media and, therefore, your PR partners would lead execution. The idea may be best executed in *paid* media, so your advertising/media agency should take the executional lead. Or it may be best to use *owned* media to put a given idea to work, so the execution of it may best be driven internally.

More than likely, it'll be a blend of all three, but the key point here is that *it depends on the idea.*

The idea must come first, and it must solve a real customer issue that hasn't been solved before. And that usually means you've found a tension to release by calling out the problem and being the solution.

As the Ariel detergent case shows, the human insight that 95% of all homes in India still had women doing all the laundry inspired an idea first, not a media plan. It drove an emotional reaction first and a rational purchase decision followed.

An empathetic view of your customers' lives means your ideas will be more well received because you're relieving a real human problem. For Ariel detergent, the empathetic tension was the existing cultural issue of gender and laundry. For Ford, the empathetic tension was that the needs of wheelchair users had never been considered by car makers. For Deluxe, the empathetic tension was that Main Street small business owners were getting pummeled by new big box retailers, and they had no help.

To find those issues, you need an empathetic view of your customers' lives first. Not a media plan.

Show Understanding

People yearn to be seen, heard, and understood. How can you show your customers that you understand them and what they're facing? How can you prove to them that you know what their challenges are? Customer service is the primary point of contact to examine this. What are people complaining about? What do they wish you did better? What issue is it that comes up most? Or what insight could you learn from your sales team? They're the ones who are on the front lines of customer experience.

Go Talk to Your Customers

For some reason, at least in my experience, there is always a seemingly artificial wall between marketers and their customers. Marketers seem to need to get them in a focus group, an unnatural environment where people are on your turf, not theirs. There are cues that exist in the "wild" that can bring up an issue you could potentially help solve. Get out there. Go talk to them where the product is sold. Go talk to customer service. Figure out any themes or issues that might give you some insight into a broader problem you could help solve.

Be Forward-Thinking

Your product team is thoroughly acquainted with the product, the category, the technology, and the innovation. Are there things they have developed that haven't come to fruition? Why? Talk to them.

You should also have insights from your company. Get to know the research and development people, the product teams, the engineers, the testing people. They'll likely all have an opinion. Learn about the problems they're trying to solve. Ask why they think those problems are so important and why they think a solution would be marketable. There may be an insight there that you could use to create or inspire a message, experience, or bigger solution.

Additionally, why not ask a group of your best customers to be on a social media panel for ideas that they either may have or want to hear about early and might appreciate helping to shape?

Many brands do in-home ethnographic research. Ask about participating in something like that. If it's been done, find the reports and look through them thoroughly. What are the trends? What are they facing? What problems can you help solve for them?

Talk to the folks who did the research. What are they seeing in your customers' lives that may not become a new product, but could become an appreciation-generating idea? Many brands do an annual brand health research study. Look through it. Ask questions. Play dumb. Get your head into the day-to-day lives of those who buy your products.

All the above can be indispensable for insightful data points. These kinds of insights can cut right to the things your customers care about and allow brands to champion something very efficiently to earn appreciation from your customers.

Be Generous

Show customers that you're not just in it for you. The more you give customers, the more they'll want to give back to you in the future. Forgive a fee. Prevent a fee. Send them a thank you gift that speaks to your shared values.

Create content that is relevant to your expertise that they'll be able to learn from and enjoy. Encourage your frontline team to write personal notes when they recognize people. Find a way to be of service.

Whirlpool started a program that installed washers and dryers in schools to address a big problem for underprivileged kids who stayed home because they didn't have clean clothes.[19] The "Care Counts" campaign is one of those ideas that is so obvious to execute. The only cost is a couple machines and a page on a website. It may not be a broad, hugely visible program, but for those who discover it and on behalf of those families want to thank the brand for the effort, it can pay off by earning reconsideration and appreciation for the brand.

Encourage a Culture of Fun

Unexpected delight always earns a deeper connection. How can you show your customers you are paying attention to what's important to them? It could be from the tone of your advertising to the culture of your company.

---

[19] Allison Slater Tate, "Schools Find One Simple Answer to Attendance Problem: Washing Machines," Today, updated August 31, 2018, https://www.today.com/parents/schools-find-one-simple-answer-attendance-problem-washing-machines-t101318.

Doing things that are surprising is one of the best ways to break through cynicism and the thousands of marketing messages people see every day. It's a whole new way to do right by them or the next customer you want to attract because it earns appreciation.

I was once on a Southwest Airlines flight that was going to leave late. The pilot came on the PA system and said, "Folks, it's no secret we're late pushing back. Just know I'm gonna fly this plane like I stole it. So, I expect an on-time arrival, assuming we don't get pulled over."

Be Purposeful

I mention this, not necessarily in the altruistic sense of "purpose-driven" marketing, more in the opportunistic way. What I mean is, some brands know who they are so well that they are nimble enough to piggyback on current events to earn attention and appreciation. After the tax cuts of 2017, Patagonia announced they would be investing their $10 million tax savings into environmental climate change causes. This made the news. And I believe it did more to earn attention and appreciation for their brand than a $10 million media buy of Patagonia TV commercials.

Be Inclusive

Nothing motivates humans more than a feeling of belonging or the aspiration to feel part of a like-minded tribe.

The most unsophisticated example? Coke wanted to "teach the world to sing," and produced a sixty second epic TV commercial to prove it, which resonated deeply with millions around the world. This iconic commercial from the '70s called "Hilltop" created a sense of global community that one could experience simply by buying a Coke. Thanks, Coke.

Be A Partner

Don't be afraid to create 1+1=3 connections. If you sell paint sprayers, partner with paint makers to make things easier for your customers to get a better result.

Perhaps start a program where you donate paint sprayers and paint to neighborhood teams who want to paint over graffiti, or even help Habitat for Humanity paint houses for deserving families. Video that. Put it on your YouTube channel. You don't need to shout kindness from the rooftops; it's much more powerful when it's organically shared and discovered by the marketplace. As the real estate example from earlier exemplified.

You could consider putting a page together on your web site that would allow appreciative people to blow your horn for you. Corona beer has a page on their site about cleaning up beach garbage. Those who discover it share it with like-valued friends. This is guaranteed to create more impact than, for example, an interruptive pre-roll ad.

Doing any of these things all comes down to your company's values and how they overlap with your customers' values. What you say to them, do for them, and what your brand solves for them must resonate, or it's a waste of time, effort, and money.

CHAPTER 15

How Appreciated Brands Win

I've spent my career helping blue chip national companies like H&R Block, Burger King, Toro, The Mayo Clinic, and others grow their business by respecting and leveraging brand meaning. Over those years I've learned: **The more a brand aspires to earn appreciation beyond its product or service, the better it does in the marketplace.**

Brands that earn Emotional Brand Appreciation are set apart in this new marketing landscape.

Most brands target potential customers with tested messaging, promotions, limited-time-offers, all the usual tactics for a brand to get attention and drive sales. Customers buy them as a matter of convenience, price, or discount, but these one-time transactions may not translate to a repeat purchase, or even any acknowledged gratitude.

Earning and Keeping Consumer Trust

We've seen a decline in public trust due to rampant misinformation, data security breaches, privacy violations, fraud, scandals, and just outright lies and corruption. Earning and keeping trust for a brand is more critical than ever.

One of the best ways to take trust seriously is to proactively *solve* problems for your customers or prospects that prove you share their values and beliefs.

Nobody earns trust by saying "trust me." You get trusted by doing what you say you'll do, performing how you say you'll perform, and making things right if something goes wrong.

Existing Values-Based Mental Channels

The signal to noise ratio is getting worse by the day. Yet we all have mental station preset tunings. We are already paying attention to things we care about.

These days almost as a survival mechanism, people ignore what they *don't* care about. But they're already paying attention to what interests them. I call these **Values Channels**. They're like different mental "stations," each comprised of the different values we are attracted to and live by. Ride on that channel and you've already got listeners tuned in.

Less Reliance on Ignorable "-er" Marketing

Remember the '70s, '80s, even '90s? Whit*er* whites? Nice! Cheesi*er* cheese puffs? Yes! Sex*ier* hair? Take my money! "-Er" marketing immediately forces you into a rational argument. It's small ball. Not to mention that an "er" after your product benefit is kind of an admission of your product's past deficiencies. (I KNEW they were holding out on the cheese!)

Appreciated Branding helps you find truly meaningful ways to matter to people.

Overcoming Mature Brand Indifference

Marketing has shifted from standing for something meaningfully different and championing it, to being principally about efficient data-driven interruption. Marketers have taken their eye off the brand. So much of the advertising out there is just mind-numbingly ignorable, and marketers are unintentionally training consumers that brands don't matter anymore.

Solving bigger problems for your customers will make your brand matter again to those you want to attract.

Neutralizing Media Proliferation

We live in a distraction economy. As marketers, we're dealing with so many new ways to reach people it's disorienting. Not just for us, but for consumers.

The very process of finding an emotional solution your customers can connect with forces you to think about it from a conceptual point of view, not a media point of view. Ideas find the media where they will best connect. They are a waypoint in this very crowded landscape. For both you, and your customers.

Make it Easier to Choose Your Brand

We now have an oversupply of perfectly good product solutions out there in just about every category. Decision fatigue among consumers has them looking for ways to simplify the choice process. A meaningful brand is a sign that says: Look here first.

When people have reason to care more about one brand over another, their options simplify, and decision fatigue goes away because they'll support the brand they appreciate.

Channel Agnostic Connection

What do you do when consumers opt out of the tech platforms you use to connect them to your message? Or when things like cookies and pixels get legislated out of existence, or their use gets significantly limited? For those brands who have built a media-agnostic, values-based relationship and are appreciated by their customers, the rented technology they're using to communicate will merely change. But emotional connections transcend *how* you connect.

In other words, your brand shouldn't just connect with your customers through wi-fi. You need a connection that will withstand the comings and goings of technology. Emotional connection is technologically agnostic.

Reverse Targeting

Championing the values your company shares with your customers is the devotion-creating, brand-strengthening circle that inspires **Reverse Targeting** – The Holy Grail of branding.

Appreciated Brands get targeted *by* customers. They are sought out because the customer sees an opportunity to live their values through their support of that brand. For example, luxury brands are reverse targeted because of the image the brand will signal about the buyer to the people they want to impress.

Reverse Targeted brands are chosen, recommended, and supported because the brand inspires more emotional loyalty – it triggers the emotions that come from feeling seen, heard, and understood.

When your brand resonates with your customers to such a great degree that *they* target *you* or, *they* advocate for *you*, or they tell friends to forsake all others for *you*, you are being Reverse Targeted. They so appreciate you that if you were to go away, they would miss you. (Think of the repercussions if Apple were to just go out of business and disappear. That would be a sad day for millions, me included.)

Customers vocally and publicly targeting businesses and brands based on the values they live by is happening more and more every day. And younger generations are doing it more than ever because they want to vote their values with their purchases.

Understandably, brands still need to be targeting consumers to create awareness and activation, but **Reverse Targeting** involves not just being the right product solution (the traditional rational USP) for a customer but the right brand (the Unique Emotional Solution) that enables their purchase to mean something more for them and the world.

For a brand to be built to last, like Steve Martin once said, "Be so good they can't ignore you."

Remember, Costco has never advertised. They don't need to. It must feel to your customers that you're so necessary, *they're* watching what *you* do without you needing to target and interrupt them.

It means you've turned your customers into messengers for you.

Generational Content Consumption Shifts

Younger generations aren't consumers in the grand old American bargain of having their "content" paid for by the dog food commercial. They didn't sign up for that. They watch mostly "on demand" content.

Therein lies the opportunity for brands today to appeal to younger generations. Appreciated Branding can, and must, be a huge part of championing change or downright helping to fix issues we all face. As a brand leader, you, and the brand you manage, can be part of solving problems as a better way to drive attention to your brand and to the performance marketing you execute to drive sales.

How Appreciated Branding Helps Business

Companies that strategically align their marketing, brand reputation management, corporate social responsibility, (CSR), environmental, social and governance (ESG), performance marketing, and social media community efforts create a force multiplier of results.

All these efforts to grow a business must complement each other. If they don't, then like an out-of-sync rowing team, you aren't capturing the best of everyone. To do that, you need to identify your core values and support them in ways that earn appreciation from your customers and employees.

Summary – How to Win

In a marketing landscape where the emotion that brands supply is frustration from constant interruption, the brand that proactively helps people will win.

Follow these four basic principles:

- Add value to your customers' or target consumers' life experiences by credibly solving an issue they face.
- Remember that how a brand makes a customer feel about their self-worth is often more important than the brand's rational, logical benefits.
- Understand that humans use brands as badges to earn positive judgment from others.
- Branding is helping, supporting, and guiding, not just interrupting. Branding is maxing out the potential of your business to endure, make more money, and drive higher margins.

Remember, the goal is not to get people to verbally acknowledge their gratitude. The goal is to be a brand that people feel appreciation for, not that people literally say "thank you" for.

CHAPTER 16

The Unique Emotional Solution

The Unique Emotional Solution is something that is inarguably desirable. It's something no other brand has claimed. And it's gonna have people feel like it's full of fresh, yet familiar stories.

Women shouldn't have to do all the laundry. (Ariel)

We need to spend more time together. (Ruavieja)

Every woman is beautiful in her own way. (Dove)

Elements of a Unique Emotional Solution:

- It's eminently recognizable. Yet it feels fresh and unsaid by anyone else.
- It creates focus and cuts out other meaningless ideas.
- The idea is a "tree trunk" of sorts, meaning all the communication branches that need to extend from it (media forms, internal campaigns, commercials, experiences, digital applications, direct mail, social media, etc.) will work in service to, and ladder up to, this main brand idea.

Honestly, it also makes things a lot more fun for those who'll work on it.

Pinning down these bigger creative ideas is hard. It takes time. It takes reflection. It takes abandoning certain ideas and letting them come back and re-find you if they're worthy. But simple insights make the creation of work underneath them easier – easier to create, sell, execute, and get results in the marketplace.

It also makes judging creative work easier. It may sound obvious, but it's often forgotten. Making a brand meaningful requires *not* doing certain things, too. Strategy, after all, is what you say *no* to.

Choosing to *say, do* and proactively *solve* things that will earn appreciation helps you bake into your strategy the avoidance of things that will be irrelevant. That is the biggest advantages of finding a Unique Emotional Solution.

Help Me Feel Meaningful

> *"We are all programmed to seek meaning and purpose and that is what unites us in social groups."*
> — Viktor Frankl, author of *Man's Search for Meaning*

Meaningfulness isn't just the secret to better marketing, it's one of the most sought-after human desires.

In his book *Man's Search for Meaning,* Viktor Frankl spelled out how he realized that to find meaning in life is to find purpose, peace, and belonging. The things that are meaningful are the things that shape our values.

APPRECIATED BRANDING

Fundamentally, when you help add real meaning to people's lives, they will feel appreciative. You're not just trying to sell them shoes, a car, or laundry detergent – you're fulfilling a deeper desire in their human experience, the need for meaning.

When you do something bigger and more meaningful, customers are more likely to remember and appreciate you in return, hence the term "a debt of gratitude." It's the power of reciprocity at work.

You could spend your marketing budget trying to convince people you care. Or you could spend some of it doing something that proves it.

CASE STUDY: H&R Block

As I reflected on the idea for Appreciated Branding, I realized I'm most proud of work in my career that aspired to be worthy of appreciation; the ideas that were helpful, inspiring, and enhanced people's lives were always the most successful, both creatively and in terms of their effectiveness.

Let me share an experience I had the first time I helped lead an advertising new business pitch.

My boss, the chief creative officer, called me down the hall to his corner office. The news wasn't good. H&R Block, one of our biggest, most high-profile accounts, just went into review. Usually, that means the agency is done. Winning as an incumbent is extremely rare.

Agencies often get this kind of news when a new CMO is hired at an existing client. Understandably, the new person wants the team *they* pick, not the team their predecessor picked.

We needed a big idea, something to galvanize this venerable company and its 3,000+ employees. And we'd be pitching against some of the best agencies in the country.

What followed was one of the most exhilarating, enjoyable, and daunting experiences I've ever had in my career. I got to see in action some of the most talented business minds, strategists, copywriters, and art directors I'd ever worked with.

The idea that my art director partner and I had come up with became the idea the agency ultimately recommended. It wasn't entirely my choice, and politically, believe me, I'd rather have had an idea that came from others on the team. But this big platform idea ended up beating some of the best agencies in North America and won the day. In looking back, I can say it marked the origins of Appreciated Branding.

"When you got H&R Block, You Got People."

Wait. I do? Oh. Wow. I'm important enough to be worthy of such resources? Thank you.

The idea made consumers feel like they had someone in their corner and a team of experts at the ready. As for the tax preparers, it helped transform them from being seen as seasonal employees to much-needed partners in their clients' success.

As an aside, I'm not saying anything about this campaign being superior to any other work done over the years for H&R Block or any other brand, for that matter. I reference this work because I'm intimately aware of every detail about its creation and its effectiveness.

With the perspective that comes with time, I can now see a core element that I hadn't realized was so important before; "You got people" was a Brand Appreciation idea.

It was a Unique Emotional Solution. Instead of the rational, product-centric "we do taxes right," it flipped the point of view to be customer-centric. It was about *them* first, not the company. It added an emotional, very desirable promise to what is essentially a transactional service.

I believe its ability to earn a thank you was one of the essential reasons it drove double digit growth every year for the three years it ran.

Finding values that overlap was the key. Block had professionals who genuinely wanted to be on their customers' side. The customers they could help had never felt like they had someone on their side. Put those two things together and it wasn't just about taxes anymore. It was about advocacy, expertise, and emotional support.

Before this campaign, walking into a strip mall H&R Block office with a shoebox of receipts was a sign of disorder, confusion, defeat, and weakness. Under the banner of "you got people," Block helped make that same activity signal to others that you were taking control and being empowered. Customers now had the means to *hire out* for a service to be done on their behalf by paid professionals.

I believe our campaign earned business for Block by earning thank yous. In fact, one of my best days as a creative director was the day our client forwarded to me an email from an H&R Block customer. In it, the customer tells the story of pulling into an H&R Block parking lot and her young daughter asking, "Mom, does this mean we have people?" The mom was so excited and appreciative about the message of worthiness her own daughter had felt from the company that she sent an email to *thank them*. That is an Appreciated Brand.

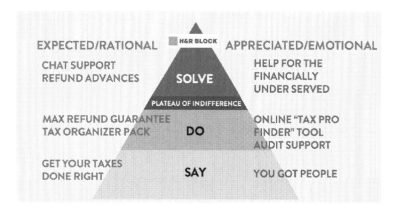

CHAPTER 17

What a Brand Appreciation Approach Requires

> *"At Patagonia, the brand IS the business."*
> — Joy Howard, former VP of Marketing, Patagonia

Leadership Must Understand the Power of Brand to Drive Growth

Show me a brand out there that you recognize, believe in, and respect, I'll show you a leadership team that knows the power of branding. They know building higher profit margins means playing the long game.

If the leadership of your company doesn't understand the power of brand belief, the power of supporting real human values, and the magnetism of providing proactive solutions, then your efforts to build a more recognized, respected, and profitable brand will likely fall on deaf ears. (Buying them a copy of this book would be a good start.)

It's About Caring

It isn't about you, it's always about your customer. You need to either offer a unique product or redefine the problem your product solves with a Unique Emotional Solution.

If you can find a movement people are already pushing toward and authentically help champion it, you'll have the wind at your back. As a former president once said, "running for president isn't about you, it's about finding the chorus. Finding the collective. In other words, you're not asking for their vote. You're asking for their help."

Inspire consumers to want to stand with you and help support the values you share. Values-based communities exist who want to be a part of something bigger. Your brand can bring energy to their efforts. For a brand to grow, you *must* give them a bigger reason that helps them help you.

This is particularly true for the millennial generation. Studies have shown they are 50% more likely to recommend a product or service to a colleague or a friend. This is why becoming an Appreciated Brand is so critical in this next marketing era.

Brand Appreciation is an outcome-based effort. It's an emotional catalyst that shakes your customers out of indifference by proactively and unexpectedly solving a problem for them. They then appreciate the brand for the action it took to help.

Brands Cannot Force Behavior

No company can make anyone, or any group, *do* anything. People ultimately do things for their own reasons, not the reasons we want them to. People buy on emotion and justify with logic.

Mark Earls in his book *Herd, How to Change Mass Behaviour by Harnessing Our True Nature*, says, "We have to admit that we cannot communicate with them in isolation or hope to persuade them. We can only influence each other, largely socially. Only by getting individuals and groups to do something for their own reasons — and even then, only by different degrees to different groups — can you try to change behavior."

There is No Failing, Only Degrees of Success.

Everyone at the company must buy in to the fact that an Appreciated Brand effort will result in either winning, or learning. It isn't necessarily something with a forecastable ROI in the manner to which everyone in the C-suite has become accustomed.

When what you're doing is intended to move hearts and minds, it's often something that takes time to take root, grow, and blossom. So, make sure you define what success looks like. And be okay with what you learn so you can apply it smartly to the next effort.

Maybe you're looking for lifts in your Net Promotor Score. Maybe you're looking for a jump in an internal employee satisfaction survey. Maybe you're going to take a pre and post Appreciation Assessment. It all depends on what the goal is, what the idea is to get you there, how and where you want to implement it, and what you're doing in support of it.

Commonalities of An Appreciated Brand Effort

There are certain things that all the cases in this book have in common:

- they have a hub, a central repository (like a website page or an X/Twitter or Threads hashtag, or a YouTube channel) around which the activity related to the idea can orbit, live and be found.

- they are frictionless and shareable, which allows for customers to easily earn cultural currency and the brand to earn attention.

- they are honest and endearing, affirming something positive and good for the human experience.

- they have a level of proactivity that puts the helping of customers first, not the selling of product.

- they solve bigger emotional problems with a Unique Emotional Solution.

- the content has a kind of "nutritional" value that isn't just meaningless interruption.

- they can involve the whole company, collaborating around real acts that can have an immediate impact for good in customers' lives.

- whether paid media should be put behind it is on a case by case, idea by idea basis. But the idea comes first in most all Brand Appreciation efforts. Media plan comes second.

CHAPTER 18

Questions to Ask to Get the Gears Turning

To help you think about adopting a Brand Appreciation approach, the following questions should be helpful:

Say: If what you offer are parity, rational product differences, using them in messaging rarely generates new interest. You need to find a Unique Emotional Solution – a way to reframe your solution. You need to find a way to stand for something unique, especially when your product doesn't.

What is the real product you're selling? Are you selling a car or are you selling freedom? Are you selling window shades or are you selling privacy? Are you selling train tickets or are you selling amazing, memorable scenery?

Notice how each of these takes a rational benefit and levels it up to something with emotional meaning.

Do: What kind of experiences can you enable or create that those who share your values would appreciate?

Sometimes, this can be a sponsorship. Stihl chainsaws helps sponsor Lumberjack Days near where I live in Minnesota.

Attendees get to see the brand in use, chewing through tree trunks like they're cottage cheese. People who attend get an experience that helps reinforce their self-identity as rough, tough, manly men. Sometimes guests post a video of one of these machines making quick work of a log to "advertise" their own rugged values, thus expanding Stihl's exposure. They may even leave the event wearing a branded cap or T-shirt.

What other experiences can your brand create that will allow your customers' values to be tangibly felt? How about a mobile car wash and detailing service for customers of your auto dealership? The key, of course, is to make sure the experience you offer lines up with the values of your customers.

Apple's biggest gaffe – some say ever – was not remembering this when they automatically uploaded a new U2 album on everyone's iPhone. It was not something that was universally appreciated.

Solve: What's a barrier, challenge, problem, or issue you can credibly support, champion, or help fix? Are there cultural issues that need to change or evolve? Is there something you can do that would make consumers want to use your brand as a badge?

How do your brand values line up with a bigger issue that you could bring attention to?

What's a big misconception, cultural tension, or proactive step your customers would appreciate you supporting that will make a difference in their lives?

As mentioned previously, a great way to find these insights, in addition to doing your own research, is through comedians. Comics are always asking why things are the way they are.

For example, Nate Bargatze is a great observer of human behavior. He often talks about the marital spats he has with his wife, to great comedic effect. Perhaps there's an appreciation-generating social media idea for a tool company to champion husbands with the hashtag #MaybeHesRight.

Alternatively, there could be one for newlywed husbands who are learning, like I did when I got married, that wives don't want you to fix their problem, they just want you to #ListenDontSolve.

The point is, there is already inherent energy behind these universal issues in our culture that hasn't been tapped.

So, finding something relatable that you can champion or help solve in your category will earn you a thank you. Tapping into that "appreciation energy" is the ultimate goal.

Know, or Determine, Your Values

What does the company stand for?

What does the company stand against?

Why was it founded?

What bigger purpose does it aspire to, or could it potentially aspire to?

What would the world be missing if it weren't in business?

What makes people proud to work there?

These values are often rooted in the company and brand's DNA and are a primary focus for leadership as they guide the company. They often present as ideals employees would claim they value beyond their paycheck. They are the standards that guide internal culture and behavior. The most impactful are those that people would say they appreciate because they, themselves, find meaning in them.

SECTION 5

WHY ALL THIS MATTERS

> *"The single largest pool of untapped resource in this world is human good intentions that never translate into action."*
>
> – Cindy Gallop, former Chairman and President, Bartle, Bogle, Hegarty US

CHAPTER 19

What Do You Want?

It's career day at your child's school. You find yourself standing at the front of the class looking at your child, who is beaming with pride that their parent is *at their school, in their class!* As you finish writing some version of "marketer" on the chalkboard, the kids' hands go up.

One curious girl asks, "What's a marketer?"

If you were to answer honestly, you'd have to say, "You know how you see ads everywhere you go? On your phone, on YouTube, on TV, by the side of the road, in the mail – pretty much interrupting everything you do? I do that. I spend lots of my company's money to get people to buy more of the things my company makes."

A young boy then asks, "How?"

"I use the data I gather from people's phones, made available to me by the surveillance tools you may not know are on your phone and computer, and then I interrupt the things you care about."

"Is that legal?" asks another kid.

"Actually, yes. Completely," you reply. "For now."

Most of us strive to become a better version of ourselves. We want to set a good example for our kids and make a difference in the lives of others. We want to be proud, honest, positive contributors.

As a CMO, brand manager, or even as a small contributor to your company's branding effort, chances are you don't enjoy spending your days in meetings choosing banner ad concepts, approving social posts, or discussing at length what word you should put in a call-to-action button.

You didn't get into this business to make decisions faster than you ever thought necessary or possible. You don't get fulfillment as a volume dealer in annoying ads that load on people's phones and slide what they're reading somewhere out of sight.

We Can Do More. You Can Do More.

The advertising business used to be much more joyful. It can be again. And it can be a much more positive force in the world than ever. Never before in history has the most powerful form of advertising ever, word of mouth, had impact through social media. It's not a "nice to do," it's the new responsibility of brands to give their customers, prospects and the world inspiration, utility, answers and solutions by using their outsized voices and influence to do things their constituents will appreciate. In this swipe past it, skip it, ignore it, hate it, interruption economy, there simply is no better way to get meaningful attention and engagement that will drive the success of brands and business. It's worth repeating Seth Godin's advice here: "Connect. Create meaning. Make a difference. Be missed."

Then

I work in advertising. I wrote that funny commercial with the racoon juggling coconuts.

Now

I work in advertising. I wrote the algorithm that allows us to follow you everywhere on the internet.

Making a Positive Difference

I believe many business leaders want to guide their companies toward real, meaningful growth with real, meaningful marketing that does more than just feed consumerism. Supplying consumers' needs with great products can be gratifying but solving our collective problems as a society can make a career in marketing infinitely more fulfilling, exciting, and rewarding.

Nobody wants to live in fear of the next quarter's sales results suddenly justifying the hiring of their replacement. Chances are you joined, or are staying with, your company because you believe in its mission, its values, or its vision for the future, and that feels purposeful to you.

Maybe you love its product. Maybe you see untapped growth you can drive. Maybe you think you can be the change agent that sets your company and brand on a new trajectory. As great as these goals are, marketers need to acknowledge that advertising and brand building has changed. In massive ways. The same old tactics may seem safe, but if you're not trying new things to win or learn from, you'll be ever more ignorable.

Employees want to be a part of a company that is well regarded and active about solving bigger problems. If, as a CMO, you want to leave a legacy, this is your opportunity.

Making a positive difference is the key to brand building in the next five years, and it's the key to a more satisfying career for marketing professionals.

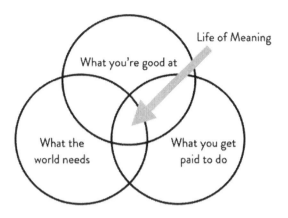

Brands That Matter Endure

As you start to move in a direction of meaning, your brand will start to matter more in the world. And all the performance marketing you do will start to earn more attention, drive better results, and grow your company.

In our bottom-line society, where doing good gets sidelined in favor of that pressing and pesky need to generate profit, we need to realign our focus towards what truly drives purchase decisions.

Increasing sales and earning gratitude are not mutually exclusive; they belong together like the wind and the sail.

I believe doing things that serve to earn gratitude for your brand will fill your financial sails and allow you to go farther and faster than you ever could on a budget-burning outboard motor. The brand that earns more gratitude from its customers will do better than the one that doesn't.

What are you doing *now* to fortify your brand so future issues are less costly and more easily forgiven? A product recall, credit card data breach, or a dreaded C-suite scandal is best defended by a more resilient, appreciated, cherished brand. Those are the brands that have people advocating for you, recommending you, sticking by you, and caring about your recovery.

Why? Because you've proven that *you* care about *them*.

Is there opportunity that presented itself five years ago that you wish you'd started then? Today, let that opportunity be the one presented by this book.

CHAPTER 20

Demand More from Your Industry

> *"Don't let others define you. Define yourself."*
> - Ginni Rometti, President & CEO, IBM

Nobody who achieves new levels of success does it by doing the same thing again and again and hoping for a different result. Let the future be your filter, not the past. If ever there was a time to embrace new ways to battle clutter that we as marketers both contribute to, and try to break through, it is now.

Allocating a small percentage of your budget to a win-or-learn approach will be the most rewarding path you could take right now.

With AI gaining more traction every day, mediocre content will become exponential. It's past time to see the bigger picture, to develop human connection and to solve problems meaningfully. Relationships are enduring and lasting. Transactions are not.

In his often-cited Stanford commencement speech, Steve Jobs crystallized the need for meaning better than probably anyone. I've edited it down slightly, but the point should be very clear:

> *Your time is limited so don't waste it living someone else's life. Don't be trapped by dogma — which is living with the results of other people's thinking. Don't let the noise of others' opinions drown out your own inner voice. And most important, have the courage to follow your heart and intuition. They somehow already know what you truly want to become.*

By now, I'm sure you've realized this book isn't about just "doing good for goodness' sake." There are plenty of books on that. And most company leaders would still say they have a purpose in place: to make money.

Fewer and fewer younger consumers will abide pure profit as a reason to support a business. My own research on this subject proved that higher gratitude drives higher emotional brand loyalty.

So, while this approach may seem like you're abandoning hard sales-generating efforts for "do good" marketing, you're not. You're taking action to prove you care about your customers.

You are making positive impressions, not interfering with people who are trying to do something else. You are solving problems in unexpected ways, and by doing so you're earning more attention than the competitor who merely interrupts without added value. You are doing more to drive long-term profit than those who merely put their message on blast and expect a response.

But more importantly, you're living with soul and purpose. As author David Brooks explained in his book *The Road to Character*, there is a difference between "résumé" virtues and "eulogy" virtues:

> *"The résumé virtues are the skills you bring to the marketplace. The eulogy virtues are the ones that are talked about at your funeral — whether you were kind, brave, honest, or faithful."*

No eulogy ever includes your net worth or the profit margin you created in consecutive quarters during a nice campaign run.

The Advertising Industrial Complex is Unsustainable

As an industry, are we creating more likable, timely, or relevant advertising? Or are we spending hundreds of millions of dollars for customers to find advertising creepier, less likable, more annoying, and more avoidable than ever? The sudden inexplicable appearance of an ad on your phone for a subject you were "just talking about!?" isn't just creepy, it can be downright scary.

A recent *New York Times* article titled "The Advertising Industry Has a Problem. People Hate Ads," by Tiffany Hsu, suggests the industry is shooting itself in the foot when it comes to connecting with the younger generation. "Many of those consumers, especially the affluent young people prized by advertisers, hate ads so much that they are paying to avoid them."[20]

---

[20] "The Advertising Industry Has a Problem: People Hate Ads," The New York Times, October 28, 2019, https://www.nytimes.com/2019/10/28/

Every time you click on a website while you're going about finding that article, video, or whatever you were looking for, an ad network makes millions of calculations to determine if they can serve you any given ad. A recent article from *Scientific American* explains what every one of us unknowingly puts into motion as we leave a digital trail of every site, click, scroll, article, and ad we looked at online:[21]

> *The ad networks are designed to shield your identity, but companies and governments are able to combine that information with other data, particularly phone location, to identify you and track your movements and online activity. More invasive yet is spyware — malicious software that a government agent, private investigator or criminal installs on someone's phone or computer without their knowledge or consent. Spyware lets the user see the contents of the target's device, including calls, texts, emails, and voicemail. Some forms of spyware can take control of a phone, including turning on its microphone and camera.*[22]

---

business/media/advertising-industry-research.html.

[21] Claire Seungeun Lee, "Online Ads Can Infect Your Device with Spyware," Scientific American, September 23, 2023, https://www.scientificamerican.com/article/online-ads-can-infect-your-device-with-spyware/.

[22] Lee, "Online Ads Can Infect."

CHAPTER 21

The Before and The After

What follows is a chart that contrasts where you may be now with where you can be as a branding and marketing professional if you follow this approach:

BEFORE	AFTER
Customer lifetime value that isn't reliable because it depends upon transient, unpredictable, and borrowed algorithms.	Customer lifetime value that is more predictable because repeat purchase is based on emotional connection and shared values, so it is media and algorithm agnositic.
A piecemeal look at the effects certain paid, earned, or owned efforts have on your brand's value.	Via the Brand Appreciation Assessment, a holistic look across the enterprise, from CSR efforts to customer service, to determine how your actions are being appreciated.
High vulnerability to competitive pressures or competitive newcomers.	Emotional loyalty that makes customers into devotees who think twice about looking elsewhere.

BEFORE	AFTER
Ever-increasing costs for paid promotion and breakthrough.	A recognized logo that is appreciated and gets attention and engagement when promoted.
Bland, transactional social channel interaction.	Inspired participation in social channels based on shared missions, causes, and values.
Profits chased via expensive promotion and price cuts.	Profit margins are more sustainable and cycle-proof due to emotional connection.
Company PR crisis if/when company or senior executive falters.	A *forgiveness bank* earned from emotional connection and appreciation.
Targeting audiences with ever-tighter budgets.	Being **Reverse Targeted** and recommended, advocated for, and talked about.
Marketing that adds no value or positive meaning to your life.	Marketing that does proactive good in the world and more easily earns attention and connection.
Mass interruption.	Breaking the **Plateau of Indifference.**
Creepiness.	Respect.
Employees who phone it in.	A team that works for a mission, not just a paycheck.
Bouncing from job to job.	Growing a meaningful business.

The Time for The Appreciated Brand Has Come

The allure of data-driven rational product messages that distract and interrupt is real, and here to stay.

As someone who believes strategy is critical to the birth of powerful, brand-building ideas, I've had the feeling that my industry was playing the same song on different instruments and believing they'd invented a new music genre. But putting all your eggs in that basket is short-sighted.

The power of owning a bigger emotional platform has been subsumed by the allure of message proximity – made possible by media proliferation.

Interruption used to be a forgivable part of watching free content. But interruption is everywhere now, and that can – and I believe *is* – causing real damage to the power of marketing.

People watch commercials on cable services they *pay to receive*. And that interruption today is at a scale humanity has never experienced.

Our industry is being driven more and more by behavioral algorithms, not the insights that inspire and influence human decision making.

Add to this the fact that there are lots of problems out there that we humans need solutions for. The time for brands and branding to positively affect our world for the better has come.

We can better earn attention by solving bigger, more worthwhile problems. If the strategic goal, as I've set forth here, is to do work that earns appreciation, then it will by default break through, get attention and inspire action.

CONCLUSION

> *"We do not inherit the earth from our ancestors.
> We borrow it from our children."*
>
> — Native American proverb

What Will You Leave Behind?

I was taught that when you borrow something, you should return it in better condition than when you received it. Borrow a car? Return it with a full tank. Borrow a cup of sugar? Replace it with a whole new pack. Camp in the mountains? Leave nothing but footprints.

How will you leave the world you're borrowing from your children? What evidence will there be that proves you cared?

You're a marketer. But before you're a marketer, you're a human being born into an incredible world where the delicate balance of life is nothing short of miraculous. Think about how extraordinary it is that we're all here, on this planet, during this time, with all the experiences we get to have around us. It's easy to take for granted.

We should all strive to do more while we're here, ensuring that we will leave things better than we found them.

As marketers – as humans living in the most opportunity rich time in human history – we've entered an amazing new age. The tools and technology we have at our disposal would have been inconceivable just a short time ago.

In this new era, where communications platforms have exploded and collided to make earning attention a huge challenge, we are presented with a whole new opportunity.

Here, I've tried to lay out a simple, potent, singular new approach that makes the job of marketing more fun, more meaningful, and more impactful from both a business perspective and for the betterment of the world.

It is now eminently easier, more efficient, and more personally satisfying to get attention for our brands by championing things that help our customers be better versions of themselves, and in so doing help advocate for our brands and do good for the broader world.

Brands and businesses will risk failure without leaders who are open to embracing new possibilities.

Smart companies will realize profit margin is being left on the table because of short-term thinking and short-term measurement.

Consumers have values that they're tuned in to. Businesses who honor, represent, and act upon their customers' values will not just get noticed, but their brands will grow stronger, more cherished, and profitable.

It's worth re-stating that the more transactional you are in the marketplace, the more your customers will see you that way and the more ignorable and replaceable you will become.

Proactively taking steps to earn the appreciation of your customers and prospects guarantees a stronger relationship and fosters a reciprocal connection where good things lead to more beneficial outcomes.

What Kind of a World Do You Want to Live In?

Customers now have a bigger voice than ever, not to mention more voices coming *at them* than ever. And yet:

People appreciate when you show you understand them.

People appreciate when your brand helps them get judged positively by others.

People appreciate when they feel a sense of belonging.

People appreciate when they get to share a discovery with others.

People appreciate when, once you've solved their problem, you help solve someone else's.

People appreciate when you add value to their lives by doing something that is useful to them.

People appreciate when they can recommend you and, in so doing, get appreciated themselves.

Supply customers with an appreciative heart and they will tell your story for you.

> **"Every action you take is a vote for the person you want to become."**
>
> — James Clear, Author

ACKNOWLEDGMENTS

This book would not have been possible without the constant support and encouragement of my family.

I also want to thank Laurie Tosto, who helped me proof and improve the book in too many ways to mention here.

All mistakes in spelling, punctuation or syntax are mine. It's very likely Laurie caught a misspelling or punctuation that I accidentally overlooked when finalizing the manuscript, so thank you to all readers who pressed on.

There are also those who've unwittingly contributed to this book by simply doing something great and admirable with their marketing. You inspired me and I am grateful and humbled by the work you did, or are doing, to market your brands.

To my friends and coworkers who have patiently listened to me talk about this "book idea" for years, I thank you for your encouragement, kindness, patience, and support. When the writer himself gets tired of hearing his own voice saying, "I'm writing a book," he knows he has probably worn some conversations thin.

To former work mates, mentors and clients who allowed me to be a part of your efforts, I am forever grateful and honored to have worked with you.

With regards to H&R Block, thank you Randy, Steve, Rich, Pete, Jessica, Lynn, Tim, Mark, Kathy, Brad, Jennifer, Joe, Ian, Carla, Allison, Paul, Gary, AJ, dMack, Amanda, John B, Kathy, Todd, Kat, Jack, Jonathan, and anyone else from the team that I may have inadvertently missed. I truly feel privileged to have worked with, and learned so much from, each of you.

ABOUT THE AUTHOR

Branding expert, speaker, executive creative director, copywriter, and author Reid Holmes has spent over three decades in some of America's biggest and best ad agencies. He's helped change the trajectory for brands like H&R Block, The Mayo Clinic, Burger King, Toro, Domino's pizza, and many others. As his kids reached high school age, Reid set a new goal, to create a more meaningful legacy. He found a simple, central theme: the best marketing seeks to earn *appreciation*. Reid believes it's time for marketing, advertising, and PR to rise and do more good for the world.

Reid is married with three kids and lives in the Twin Cities.

THANK YOU FOR READING!

I'm here for you.
Would you take a moment
to be here for me?

I need your input to make the next version of this book, and my future books, better.

Please leave me an honest review on Amazon letting me know what you thought of the book.

I really appreciate all your feedback, and I love hearing what you have to say. I will no doubt find things I can fix in future versions, and with your help those fixes will be more comprehensive.

If you did find any typos or needed corrections, please email me directly at reid@appreciatedbranding.com and I will fix it for the next release.

Thank you. I appreciate you.

Reid

Made in United States
Orlando, FL
25 November 2024

54424033R00100